LONDON
HERITAGE PUBS

An inside story

Geoff Brandwood & Jane Jephcote

Published by the Campaign for
Real Ale Ltd
230 Hatfield Road
St Albans
Herfordshire AL1 4LW

www.camra.org.uk/books

ISBN 978-1-85249-247-2

A CIP catalogue record for this book
is available from the British Library

Printed and bound in China
by 1010 Printing International Ltd

Managing Editor: Simon Hall
Project Editor: Marcus Hardy
Editorial Assistants: Emma Haines;
Katie Hunt
Design: Ian Midson
Index: Jane Coulter
Photography: Geoff Brandwood
(except where otherwise stated)
Cover: James Hall
Head of Marketing: Louise Ashworth

DEDICATION
For Jean and Robert with
thanks for their patience

Finding your way around this book

The pub entries in this book are arranged into seven main
areas, reflecting the London postal boundaries. Central London
includes EC1 to EC4, WC1 and WC2. The other six areas have
their pubs listed in numerical order (E1, E3, etc) followed in
alphabetical order by the outlying areas that do not have
London postal numbers (e.g. Ilford, IG1; Romford, RM1 etc).
Note that some regions straddle more than one postal district.

Listed status and CAMRA National Inventory (NI) classification

As you will discover, the reason these pubs are in this guide
is that they retain important historic features and interest.
As such, many are listed under the Planning (Listed Buildings
and Conservation Areas) Act 1990 and/or appear in CAMRA's
*National Inventory of Pub Interiors of Outstanding Historic Impor-
tance* (*National Inventory* or NI for short). The listed status and NI
classification of each pub is given at the beginning of its entry.

In England there are three types of listed status (in descending
order of 'importance'): **Grade I**, **Grade II*** and **Grade II**. (*See
feature, p.182.*) CAMRA's *National Inventory* comes in two parts:
Part One (comprising the most intact interiors) and **Part Two**.
(*See feature, p.190.*)

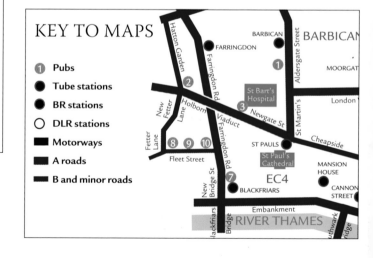

Contents

CAMPAIGN FOR REAL ALE

Biographies

Geoff Brandwood has a PhD in architectural history and a special interest in the Victorian age. He was Chairman of the Victorian Society from 2001-2007. Horrified by the wholesale disappearance of historic pub interiors in recent years, he is part of CAMRA's Pub Heritage Group. He is co-author of English Heritage's best-selling *Licensed to Sell: The History and Heritage of the Public House* (2004).

Jane Jephcote's interest in London's historic pub interiors began in 1991 when she joined CAMRA's London Pubs Group of which she is now Chair. The Group promotes the preservation of London's pub heritage and good pub design. Jane organises and leads crawls of pubs with interiors of note all over Greater London and was co-author with Geoff Brandwood of *The CAMRA Regional Inventory for London: Pub Interiors of Special Historic Interest* (2004).

Introduction

This book brings you London's most important historic pub interiors. They are a hugely varied collection ranging from late Victorian extravaganzas, replete with lavish decoration, to simple, basic street-corner locals. The one thing they have in common, though, is interiors with genuine historic layouts and/or features, which we hope will make a visit both interesting and enjoyable. By 'historic' we mean interiors still surviving from before the great wave of refitting that began in the 1960s and which has transformed the character of the vast majority of pubs throughout the land. It is this wholesale transformation which explains why this book contains a mere 156 entries when Greater London contains something in the order of 5,500 pubs spread over its 33 boroughs and 609 square miles. These are precious survivals that deserved to be cherished.

There are some famous London pubs which have a long history and which you may be surprised do not feature here. The point is that just because a pub has been around a long time, this does not mean its interior has any heritage value if the place was gutted within the last few decades. It could well be that Charles Dickens found inspiration there in the 1830s but,

if it has just been opened up and turned into a café-style bar with pastel paintwork and soft seating, it won't appear here.

This guide grew out of the Campaign for Real Ale's (CAMRA's) concern about this rapid disappearance of our pub heritage and the major survey it initiated to identify and to campaign for the survival of the best remaining examples. Following the resulting publication of its *National Inventory of Pub Interiors of Outstanding Historic Importance* (*National Inventory* or NI for short), CAMRA has moved on to produce more detailed guides for other parts of the country. The first of these was the *Regional Inventory for London*, published in 2004, which formed the foundation for this new book. All the pubs have been revisited, new ones discovered, all the descriptions revised and extended, and new photography undertaken.

Although this book is published by CAMRA, real ale is not a requirement for inclusion although the majority of the pubs do sell it. Nor are qualities like atmosphere and friendliness although, as with most pubs, you will be made most welcome, especially if you say why you've taken the trouble to come and say a few nice words about the pub. So the criterion for inclusion is simply the existence of a genuine historic setting in which to enjoy what people have enjoyed in pubs for centuries – a drink, good conversation and perhaps a bite to eat as well.

TEN PUBS NOT TO MISS

Although we authors think you would be well-advised to visit all the pubs in this book, that's something of a tall order. So, which of them form a Top Ten – pubs where we know you'll enjoy really special, important historic interiors (and also a drop of good real ale)?

Princess Louise

Red Lion

Cittie of Yorke

Eastbrook

PRINCESS LOUISE, HOLBORN (p13).
This pub has a fantastic interior from the late-Victorian golden age of pub building. What makes it even more special is, paradoxically, modern: the reinstallation of the screens that used to divide it up into small drinking compartments. Just the sort of thing our ancestors loved.

CITTIE OF YORKE, HOLBORN (p9).
Go to the rear bar. You might be forgiven for thinking you are in a centuries-old mighty Tudor hall. But what surrounds you was created as a piece of nostalgia in the 1920s. The great vats are a reminder of the former owners, George Henekey & Company.

RED LION, ST JAMES'S (p167).
This magical, tiny pub is a *tour de force* from the great age of pub-building just before 1900. It's packed with beautiful mirrors which make it seem bigger than it really is.

BLACK FRIAR, BLACKFRIARS (p28).
This Victorian pub was remodelled from 1905 with a witty, decorative scheme celebrating the Dominican friars who lived nearby. The goings-on are, to say the least, a bit fanciful but the end result is unique.

EASTBROOK, DAGENHAM (p137).
Perhaps a pilgrimage to the outer reaches of East London, but this is one of the best surviving 1930s estate pubs anywhere in the country. The Walnut Room and the Oak

Room, each so named for self-explanatory reasons, are intact survivors from the 1930s when the pub was built.

Black Friar   **Prince Alfred**

FORESTER, EALING (p67).
One of the best pubs designed by the busy pub architect Nowell Parr (see p47). This pub of 1909 has a lovely Edwardian exterior and a multi-roomed interior which shows the shift from extravagant Victorian design to the more restrained Edwardian style. If trekking out here you might care to partake of the excellent Thai cuisine that's on offer.

SALISBURY, HARRINGAY (p106).
A splendiferous establishment from the great age of pub-building around 1900, recently and lovingly restored to its former glory and now offering good cuisine. This is Victorian pub-building at its most spectacular.

Forester

PRINCE ALFRED, MAIDA VALE (p55).
A unique survival of a multi-compartmented pub with screens dividing up the spaces around a late Victorian serving area. Service doors allow access between one compartment and the next. Now a classy dining pub.

FALCON, BATTERSEA (p177).
Right by bustling Clapham Junction station this 1887 pub-cum-hotel has one of the longest bar counters in the country. Stained glass and multiple rooms complete the picture of a fine late-Victorian drinking establishment.

Salisbury

OLDE CHESHIRE CHEESE, HOLBORN (p30).
The tiny front bar at the Cheshire Cheese is a real step back in time with, probably, some of the oldest woodwork of any pub in the country. The panelling and seating may even date back to the rebuilding after the Great Fire of London in the late 17th century.

Falcon   **Olde Cheshire Cheese**

Above: **The main bar of the Cittie of Yorke**

Left: **Art Deco main bar of the Duke of the York, complete with its original patterned lino**

CENTRAL

WC1 to WC2

CITTIE OF YORKE ①

22 High Holborn, Holborn, WC1V 6BN
020 7242 7670.
Grade II listed.
Tube: Chancery Lane.
NI Part One.
Real ale.

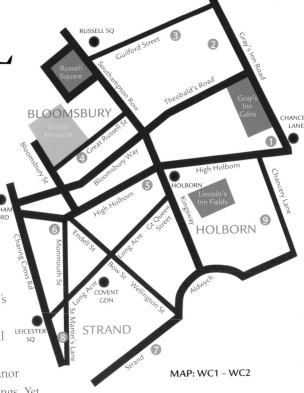

MAP: WC1 – WC2

A visit to the main bar of the Samuel Smith's Cittie of Yorke is a pub experience like no other. You enter a mighty 'olde Englishe' hall with a high roof, massive wine vats and a high-level window where the lord of the manor might have once presided over the proceedings. Yet, this pub is a rebuild of 1923-4 – not 1523 – in a deliberately nostalgic and evocative style. The frontage is narrow (the pub stretches far back, probably reflecting an ancient property site) and has graceful 16th-century architectural details. At the front, the bar is fairly unexceptional and has wall panelling.

The back room of the pub is long and narrow, with the servery on the left and above it a shelf supporting huge vats. These are a reminder that the pub was rebuilt by wine merchants George Henekey & Company who also developed a chain of pubs. The vats are said to have been in use up to World War II. Across from the servery there are seven small carrels designed for more intimate and discrete enjoyment. This arrangement was unique among British pubs (but popular in Northern Ireland) until its reinvention in, for example, some Wetherspoon's pubs. There are three more such booths at the back of the pub on the left. Also, have a look at the huge triangular stove which is said to date from 1815 and, unusually, has a flue which goes downwards to exit the building. The brick cellars from the previous building on the site form the Cellar Bar.

The pub was taken over, along with the rest of the Henekey chain, in 1979 by Yorkshire brewers Samuel Smith who changed the name to the Cittie of Yorke (evoking a long-vanished pub

WHAT COUNTS AS A PUB?

Not quite as easy as it might sound. There's plenty of room for hair-splitting! We are treating a 'pub' as any licensed premises with free entry where draught beer (real ale or otherwise) is available and where you can drink without being required to eat. Hence clubs, pure restaurants, hotel bars open only to hotel guests and wine or cocktail bars with bottled beers only are all excluded from this book.

Above: **Exterior of the Cittie of Yorke**

Below: **The Duke of York, by architect D E Harrington, photographed in the late 1930s.** *Andrew Davis Collection*

across the road in Staple Inn). The outside signage and hanging ironwork at the back of the pub, the stained glass in the window overlooking the main bar and the copper cartouches are all Smith's work and are very well done.

History down the road: At 1-4 Holborn Bars is Alfred Waterhouse's magnificent red terracotta tour de force of 1886 commissioned by the Prudential Assurance Company.

DUKE OF YORK ❷

7 Roger Street, Bloomsbury, WC1N 2PB
020 7242 7230.
Not listed.
Tube: Russell Square.
NI Part One.
Real ale.

An Art Deco treasure dating from 1938. This corner pub, now with a major focus on good food, is part of an offices and flat development and, like the rest of the block, has characteristic 1930s detailing and metal windows.

The pub isn't big but has two unequally sized rooms which, incredibly, have retained their original work almost completely, and show what many inter-war pubs looked like before modern changes. Decoration is pared down to a minimum and the fittings are sleek and undemonstrative. The counters have plain vertical surfaces and the bar-backs are simple and functional. Perhaps the most surprising feature is the original lino flooring with red, black and buff blocky patterns in both rooms. Even the corridor steps down to the gents' have the original red lino.

In the smaller rear room is an original brick fire surround and several Art Deco mirrors. The most prominent feature here is a series of small open drinking booths with timber and reeded glass partitions between them. The similar seating in the larger bar, however, looks like a later addition, perhaps from around 1960 when the Double Diamond window glass must have gone in. Don't miss the loos, which are also amazingly intact. The Duke of York is primarily aimed at diners although part of the larger bar welcomes drinkers too.

History in the area: In nearby Doughty Street Charles Dickens lived from 1837 to 1839 at number 48. It is now the Dickens House Museum and is his only surviving London home.

LAMB ❸

94 Lamb's Conduit Street, Bloomsbury, WC1N 3LZ
020 7405 0713.
Grade II listed.
Tube: Russell Square.
Real ale.

Housed in a Georgian building, this Young's pub has long been popular with real ale drinkers. Outside, things to note are the magnificent, swirly cast-iron lamp bracket and the two-tone green tiling which probably dates from the Edwardian era.

Inside, the pub is now a single space but would once have been divided up into several small compartments. The most famous feature at the Lamb is the double range of snob screens set on either side of the counter. The three-sided bar counter is late-Victorian or Edwardian.

On the right is a small snug area with etched glass, some of it clearly reused rather than new – most obviously the panel stating 'saloon' – and which would originally have been in a door. At the rear left is a sunken area with some simple wall panelling. Other old fittings are the matchboard panelled ceiling and some slender columns with foliage capitals supporting the upper floors. Don't miss the polyphon, the Victorian mechanical equivalent of a juke box in the right-hand part – a donation to the pub's charity will allow you to hear it play.

History nearby: Turning left and left again out of the pub you will find a stone plaque on the site of a former lost water supply declaring 'Lams Conduit the Property of the City of London this Pump is Erected for the Benefit of the Publick'.

Above: **Elaborate sign outside the Lamb**

MUSEUM TAVERN ❹

49 Great Russell Street, Bloomsbury, WC1B 3BA
020 7242 8987.
Grade II listed.
Tube: Tottenham Court Road.
Real ale.

As the name suggests, this pub is right opposite the entrance to the British Museum. It claims a long history stretching back into the 18th century and was originally known as the Dog and Duck but changed its name with the arrival of the museum.

Below: **Front façade of the Museum Tavern**

The building we see today is a rebuilding of 1855 by the architect, William Finch Hill. Big changes took place in 1889 with a refitting by Wylson and Long for the then landlord, George Blizzard. The ornate bar-back and tapering counter survive as does one original mirror advertising Watney's Imperial Stout (the other mirrors are from later).

The four outside doors show how the interior was divided up in former days. You can still see the names 'public bar', 'private bar', 'saloon' and 'luncheon buffet' in the door and window glass. In fact there were five bars in all: they became three in 1935 and these, sadly, became one in the 1960s. The square panelling of the ceiling adds much to the character of the pub. There are two panels of stained glass at the rear of the pub. Unfortunately, the splendid fireplace at the far end has been compromised by the addition of inappropriate cabinets and tiles.

History across the street: The British Museum was established in 1753 to house the collections of the scientist and physician, Sir Hans Sloane and opened to the public in 1759 in Montagu House on the site of the present building. The present building, designed by Sir Robert Smirke, with its magnificent façade facing the pub, was begun in 1823 and eventually opened to the public in 1852. The famous Round Reading Room, designed by Smirke's younger brother, Sydney, was added in 1854-7 and was home to the British Library until 1997 which then relocated to a site near St Pancras station.

PRINCESS LOUISE ⑤

208-9 High Holborn, Holborn, WC1V 7BW
020 7405 8816.
Grade II* listed.
Tube: Holborn.
NI Part Two.
Real ale.

This is one of *the* must-visit historic pubs, remarkable both for its sumptuous late Victorian work and an amazing modern restoration. But let's start back in 1872 with the then owners, W and H H Whale who applied to expand their Holborn pub at number 209 into number 208 next door. It is from this scheme that the florid iron columns and, no doubt, the swirly-patterned ceiling date. Then, in the 1890s, Henry Whale (son of H H) did

<< *LEFT HAND PAGE*
Above: **Interior of the Museum Tavern**
Below: **Recently restored interior of the Princess Louise**

Above: **Princess Louise façade**
Below: **Princess Louise – the gents'**

what countless other pub owners were doing at the time and went for an ambitious upgrade.

This work may have proceeded in two stages, the first, around 1892, involving magnificent glass supplied by the Kennington firm of R Morris & Son who obligingly signed their work, and tiling by W B Simpson & Sons of St Martin's Lane who may have been in overall charge under the otherwise unknown architect Arthur Chitty. The tiles and glass, ranged down the side walls, are among the best anywhere. At the rear left and down the stairs are stained glass panels representing music, drama and painting.

Then comes a plan from 1897 (this is displayed on the stairs) signed by architects Bird & Walters and changed slightly on execution, showing small screened-off booths surrounding a peninsula-style stillion. This still survives with arches, shelves, a dumb waiter, four-sided clock and yet more tilework. But in the early to mid-20th century the screens came out and things remained like that until 2007 when the present owners, Yorkshire brewers, Samuel Smith, under the architect Michael Drain, did a magnificent thing – they put them back. They have thus returned the ground floor to more or less how it was a century ago. The glass in the screens is modelled on the design of the one-remaining original door panel (on the right). The lovely mosaic floors in the corridors are from the 2007 scheme.

Last but not least – the gents'. They are a piece of lavatorial magnificence only exceeded in the Philharmonic pub in Liverpool and are proudly signed by their makers, J Tylor & Sons of London and Sydney.

ANGEL ⑥

61 St Giles High Street, Covent Garden, WC2H 8LE
020 7240 2876
Not listed.
Tube: Tottenham Court Road.
Real ale.

This Samuel Smith pub comes in two very separate halves. The original part from c.1900 is on the right but expanded later into the property on the left. The most striking feature is on the far right, a former carriage entrance which has now been turned into an extra room with seating. It is awash with tiling, even on

Above: **Angel interior**
Below: **Red brick exterior of the Angel**

the ceiling. A disembodied hand points the way to the 'saloon bar 2nd door'. This is a small snug which has been recreated by owners, Samuel Smith of Tadcaster as part of their excellent refit in the 1990s. The screen between the carriageway and the bars is original and has beautiful swirling designs in etched glass. The bar counter in the right-hand part of the pub is original but the bar-back is a replacement.

The left-hand room would seem to have been incorporated into the pub in about 1930 judging by the sleek style of the counter: the seating is quite modern. At the time of writing it was possible to detect a former opening between the two main rooms – it was filled in during the 1990s and returned the pub to having separate rooms once more.

History nearby: A little to the west is the fine church of St Giles-in-the-Fields, rebuilt in 1731-3 to designs by Henry Flitcroft. As a complete contrast there is Centre Point, the famous 34-storey tower of 1959-67, designed by Richard Seifert & Partners, and which, at the time, aroused fierce emotions as a symbol of opportunistic property speculation.

Above: **Coal Hole exterior**

COAL HOLE ⑦

91 The Strand, Strand, WC2R 0DW
020 7379 9883
Grade II listed.
Tube: Charing Cross, Covent Garden, Leicester Square.
Railway Station: Charing Cross.
Real ale.

A stunning piece of 'olde Englishe' revival as employed, rather later, at the even more stunning Cittie of Yorke (p9). The pub is part of the Savoy Court complex built in 1903-4 to designs by a well known Edwardian architect T E Collcutt.

Expense was not spared in creating a lofty, beamed, L-shaped drinking hall whose main decorative theme is the celebration of the fruit of the vine. In a massive, deep frieze there are decorative young ladies collecting grapes in an agreeable state of undress. At the rear of the pub is an exuberant terracotta fireplace decorated with juicy bunches of grapes and an escutcheon with the uplifting motto *'convivium moderatum atque honestum'* (loosely translated as an exhortation to honesty and what we now refer to as 'responsible drinking'). The bar-back with

RIGHT HAND PAGE >>

Above: **Coal Hole interior as seen from the mezzanine floor**

Below: **Fine wood and glass exterior of the Salisbury**

Above: **The Salisbury's main bar**

Below: **Bronze lamps in the Salisbury**

its flat-arched openings and simply panelled counter is original though the obtrusive gantries stuck on the corners are an unpleasant modern addition. Do go upstairs to the mezzanine floor from where you can get a bird's eye view of this spectacular pub and its sumptuous features.

The pub claims to take its name from being a popular hostelry for London coal heavers who used to fuel the city before the arrival of natural gas. There is also a small, windowless snug in the basement which purports to be the pub's coal hole.

History nearby: In the area the Lamb and Flag, tucked away in Rose Street, is worth a visit. It has old panelling, a Victorian bar counter and a partitioned-off space at the rear. Over the left-hand doorway an arrow points to the 'public bar' to the right – clear evidence that there was a separation of the front part into two bars (removed, sadly, in the last couple of decades).

SALISBURY ⑧

90 St Martin's Lane, Covent Garden, WC2N 4AP
020 7836 5863
Grade II listed.
Tube: Leicester Square.
NI Part Two.
Real ale.

This is one of the very best pubs in Central London to appreciate the glitz and glamour of the late-Victorian great pub boom. It's in a tall red-brick building on a corner site in the heart of Theatreland and is often very busy (but has a good variety of real ales). It opened in 1898 and takes its name from the Marquess of Salisbury who was three times Prime Minister of Britain between 1885 and 1901. His family once owned the freehold on the property.

The 'SS' in the lavish window glass stands for the original name 'Salisbury Stores', 'stores' being a not uncommon tag in pub names at the time. The fine glasswork continues within the pub, especially in the serving area. There is also a good sense of how pubs around 1900 were divided up – you can see the various entrance doorways and a surviving glazed screen creating a small snug down the St Martin's Court side. Other features to note are an original island bar counter (partly topped with white marble), and what are always said to be original bronze lamp

Above: **Exterior of the much-loved Seven Stars**

Below: **Interior of the Seven Stars**

holder statuettes of girls out hunting with a dog and a quiverful of arrows: these sit on top of the divisions between the seats on the main bar. In contrast to the glorious Victorian glass it is a sad fact that the modern etched work in the main bar and rear room look quite cheap and nasty.

History over the road: The mighty 2,358-seater Coliseum Theatre, home to the English National Opera, was designed by the great theatre architect, Frank Matcham, for entrepreneur Sir Oswald Stoll and opened in 1904.

SEVEN STARS ⑨

53-4 Carey Street, Holborn, WC2A 2JB
020 7242 8521
Grade II listed.
Tube: Temple, Chancery Lane.
Real ale.

A small, famous and much-loved free house in the heart of legal London. The frontage bears the date 1602 but the building itself probably dates only from the 1680s. The core of the pub is the part with doors embellished with etched and gilded glass declaring 'private counter' (on the left) and 'general counter' (right). These names are probably unique, certainly in the experience of the writers, and correspond to the more commonly used 'private bar' and 'public bar'. So there were evidently two separate areas fronting on to a common servery and divided, no doubt, by a timber screen.

The counter (a plain affair) and bar-back are Victorian and the coloured advertising panels in the head of the latter are typical of the period around 1870-1890. The pub expanded into a right-hand area and recently has experienced further growth on the left into the next-door building to form a cosy drinking area called the 'Wig Box'. Imagine the pub without these extensions and you can get a sense of just how small it was in Victorian days. There are three fine old advertising mirrors.

History across the street: Facing the Seven Stars is the massive bulk of the Royal Courts of Justice. Erected in 1871-82 to designs by the architect G E Street, the complex is described in the *Buildings of England* volume for Westminster as 'the greatest secular monument of the Gothic Revival in London after the Houses of Parliament.'

EC1 to EC4

HAND & SHEARS ❶

1 Middle Street, Smithfield,
EC1A 7JA
020 7600 0257
Grade II listed.
Tube: Barbican.
NI Part One.
Real ale.
Closed weekends.

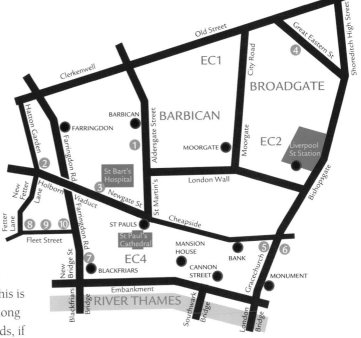

MAP: EC1 – EC4

Popular with office workers at lunchtime and early evening, this is one of the best-kept secrets among City pubs and looks as hundreds, if not thousands, of plainly furnished London pubs did a century ago. The building probably dates from 1830 with later fittings. The pub name comes from Bartholomew Fair when the Lord Mayor cut the first cloth at what was England's greatest cloth fair (the fair was granted a royal charter in 1133 but was suppressed in 1855 amid fears about public disorder).

The corner entrance has an unusual pair of curved doors. There are in fact several doorways, each leading into a separate drinking space around the central servery. Two of these spaces are named in the door glass which looks like a refitting (along with the window glazing) from the 1930s. So we have, on the right, the 'saloon' and left of this is a cosy little 'private bar'. A sensitive refurbishment in 1989 expanded the gents' slightly into the rear bar, installed the diagonal shelving over the servery and replaced the iron columns but the overall character of the pub was carefully kept.

Nearby: The Fox & Anchor, 115 Charterhouse Street, near Smithfield Market, is worth a visit for its gorgeous Art Nouveau ceramic frontage and entrance. It is one of those pubs which keeps extraordinary hours for market workers, opening at 7:00 in the morning for breakfast (now served at gastropub prices!).

History in the area: To the west of the Hand & Shears lies St Bartholomew's church, the oldest in London and part of an Augustinian priory founded in 1123. The stern, deeply impressive choir dating from the 12th-century church still survives.

Above: **Curved entrance doors to the Hand and Shears**

Below: **Hand and Shears snug**

HOW OLD IS OLD?

To the oft-asked question 'which is the oldest pub in the country?' there is no shortage of answers. London, mercifully, does not enter the contest, which does manage to produce some absurd pre-Conquest claims from imaginative pub-owners as far afield as Gloucestershire, Cambridgeshire and Yorkshire. Despite various spurious claimants, nobody can say which is the oldest pub in London, so we'll simply let the matter rest there. But, beyond the myth and the hype, drinking establishments have been with us for a long time even though the physical traces have been lost. Our Roman visitors had their equivalents of the pub and, after their departure, Saxon England also had places for public drinking. Medieval London, with some 30,000 to 40,000 people, was said by 1309 to have had 354 taverns (which mainly sold wine) and over 1,330 places brewing and retailing ale. The larger ones were important places in the life of the city and it was from one of these

inns, the Tabard, that Chaucer set his pilgrims off on their story-telling journey to Canterbury. Samuel Pepys's diaries, dating from the 1660s, show how drinking establishments added to the quality of his life while drinking dens often provide the backdrop to low life in the work of Dickens.

But in what we can see today, how old is old? Surprisingly, not very, if we compare pubs with the age of, say, our churches, castles or great country houses. As places of pleasure and entertainment, pubs have been constantly updating themselves and, although a building itself may be centuries old, pub interiors hardly ever predate the mid-19th century. Some of the woodwork in the old bar at the Olde Cheshire Cheese, Holborn (p30), and in a room at the George, Southwark (p139), might conceivably go back to the rebuilding of these venerable pubs in the late 17th century, but this is totally exceptional. The earliest clearly datable fitting in London is the sumptuous High Victorian barback at the Victoria, Bayswater (p43) where the clock is, very thoughtfully, inscribed 1864. It is actually very hard to date pub fittings accurately on stylistic grounds because the firms responsible were rarely at the cutting edge of fashion (and their clients even less so) and would reuse the same type of designs for decades on end.

Inside the original bar at the Old Cheshire Cheese, Holborn (p30)

The High Victorian bar-back dating from 1864 at the Victoria, Bayswater (p43)

Above: **Alley outside the Olde Mitre**
Below: **Olde Mitre, 1930s interior**

OLDE MITRE ❷

1 Ely Court, Ely Place, Holborn, EC1N 6SJ
020 7405 4751
Grade II listed.
Tube: Chancery Lane.
NI Part One.
Real ale.
Closed weekends.

Finding this vibrant, historic pub in a tiny alley between Hatton Garden and Ely Place is a test of pub-going initiative but success will be rewarded by several regular ales plus a guest. It is said to have been founded in 1546 to minister to the servants of the Bishop of Ely who had his London residence in the vicinity. It was rebuilt at the end of the 18th century but the interior is a remodelling of around 1930 with lots of panelling in the then-fashionable Tudor style. There are two rooms (both called 'lounge bar') either side of a central servery a small, cosy one at the front and a larger one at the back. Off the latter is an intimate little snug, now named 'Ye Closet'. The upstairs 'Bishop's Room' was fitted out about 1990. The gents' can only be entered from outside – how rare is that in a London pub?

History on the spot: Elizabeth I's Chancellor, Sir Christopher Hatton, built himself a fine house on this site. Hatton House, however, had gone by 1720 and the link with the Diocese of Ely ceased in 1772 when Ely Place passed to the Crown. (Unusually the site is still Crown property and therefore outside the jurisdiction of the City of London).

VIADUCT TAVERN ❸

126 Newgate Street, Smithfield, EC1A 7AA
020 7600 1863
Grade II listed.
Tube: St Paul's.
Railway station: City Thameslink.
Real ale.
Closed weekends.

This popular Fuller's pub sweeps majestically round the corner of Newgate Street and Giltspur Street. It was built in 1874 but the wonderful fittings we see today are due to a remodelling by

Arthur Dixon in 1898-1900 at the height of the *fin de siècle* pub-building boom. The separate drinking areas (as indicated by the multiple outside doors) have gone but there is an amazing amount of excellent decoration. The etched, gilded and cut-glass panels at the rear are truly spectacular and are the equal of the work at the Princess Louise (p13). Another highlight is the small, glazed-in office in the rear of the serving area that was used for conducting the administration of the pub. It has fine etched glass and delicate woodwork. Delicate is also the word to describe the small stillion in the middle of the servery with its arched woodwork and ornamented glass. The ceiling too (which probably dates from the original build in 1874), with its swirling relief panels, is a also a fine sight. Less attractive are the three paintings of languid ladies, signed 'Hal', on the right-hand wall, who, apparently, represent agriculture, commerce, industry and art. They are set in an arcade with extensive marble work. Don't miss the bar counter itself which has unusual, bold, arched decoration. A final curiosity is the heavily carved, sliding door at the rear to the private quarters above.

History underneath: In the cellars are remains of cells from Newgate Prison, notorious for its appalling conditions until it was rebuilt in 1770-8. If the pub isn't too busy, do ask to have a look at them. The prison was demolished in 1902 to make way for the Central Criminal Court (aka the Old Bailey).

Above: **Viaduct Tavern interior detail**

Below: **Late-19th-century interior of the Viaduct Tavern**

GRIFFIN ❹

93 Leonard Street, Shoreditch, EC2A 4RD
020 7739 6719.
Not listed
Tube: Old Street, Liverpool Street, Shoreditch.
Railway stations: Liverpool Street, Old Street.
Real ale.

The Griffin we have today is actually two buildings that have been knocked into one pub. The older part stretches down Ravey Street and has some typical detailing from about 1870. The later part, on the corner, has some distinctive tiled panels and must date from later in the 19th century. Then, between the wars, along came the brown tile refacing of all the ground-floor walls by Meux's Brewery to promote their wares – they brewed on the site of the Dominion Theatre, Tottenham Court

Road until 1921, then moved to Nine Elms where brewing ceased in 1964.

All the internal partitioning has gone but the Victorian counter remains, as does the matchboard panelling that covers the ceiling. But the feature of most interest is the back fitting behind the bar with a series of unusual, highly ornamented wooden columns, a number of original mirrors and a fancy cornice above.

JAMAICA WINE HOUSE ⑤

St Michael's Alley, Cornhill, EC3V 9DS
020 7929 6972
Grade II listed.
Tube and DLR: Bank.
Real ale.
Closed weekends.

Known colloquially as the Jam Pot, this tucked-away pub is generally busy with local City workers at lunchtimes and early evening. It lies up a short alleyway off Cornhill beside St Michael's church – look out for the massive, iron-bracketed lantern with the pub's name. The pub is part of a red brick and sandstone block rebuilt in 1885 to designs by architect Banister Fletcher (don't fall for the 'Built 1652' notices!).

The intriguing rectangular layout is divided up into four by three screens set at right angles to the counter. Originally there would have been no link between the two left-hand and the two right-hand compartments. The distinction between the two parts is emphasised by completely different ceiling treatments: that on the left, unusually, has panels of ceramic or enamelled metal. It is almost as though the pub was built in two stages but there is no evidence of this in the fabric of the building. The screens themselves are fine pieces of mahogany woodwork, decorated with square panels and some glazed parts.

The counter is original but has been altered in the right-hand area. The bar-back and seating are modern.

History on the spot: This was the site of England's first coffee house, established by a Turk, Pasqua Rosee, and in existence by 1654. Coffee houses played an important part in the social and business lives of the country's better-off urban population in the 18th century. This one became the Jamaica Coffee House in 1674, changing into a wine house in 1869.

Below: **Interior of the Jamaica Wine House**

Above: **Tiled exterior of the Griffin**

Right: **Jamaica Wine House, known locally as the Jam Pot**

LAMB TAVERN ⑥

10-12 Leadenhall Market, The City, EC3V 1LR
020 7626 2454
www.thelambtavern.co.uk
Grade II* listed.
DLR: Bank.
Tube: Bank, Monument, Mansion House, Cannon Street.
Railway stations: Cannon Street, Fenchurch Street.
Real ale.

<< *LEFT HAND PAGE*

Above: **Lamb Tavern exterior**
Below left: **Warren of rooms in the Lamb Tavern cellar**
Below right: **Tiling detail in the Lamb**

The Lamb is at the heart of the echoing splendour of Leadenhall Market, rebuilt in 1880-1 to the designs of Horace Jones, architect and surveyor to the City of London. Once bustling with market traders, porters and their customers, the market is now more a series of gentrified boutiques but its pub is still a vibrant place to visit.

Apart from the architecture, there are several historic features. The external glazing has lots of etched glass including a large corner panel with the words 'W Pardy Wine and Spirit Merchant' and door glass naming the former rooms within. Just inside the right-hand doors is a large tiled panel from the prolific firm of W B Simpson & Son, helpfully dated March 1889. As the inscription says, it shows Sir Christopher Wren in 1671 explaining (for some reason best known to him) his plans for the Monument to those gathered around, including a puzzled lady in a carriage attended by her black servant boy. The cellar bar is a warren of spaces under depressed, red-brick jack-arches and is notable for its cream and green tiling. The rest of the fittings and arrangements are modern, including the mezzanine floor.

History all around: The market, named after a mansion here, was one where people from outside London were allowed to sell poultry and cheese in the 14th century. The house and estate were sold to the City Corporation in 1411 and in 1445 the newly built granary was declared a general market. Both mansion and market were lost in the Great Fire (1966). The market was rebuilt around three large courtyards, which survived until the present buildings were erected. Their design owes much to the great Galleria in Milan, built in 1865-77.

BLACK FRIAR 7

174 Queen Victoria Street, Blackfriars, EC4V 4EG
020 7236 5474
Grade II* listed.
Tube and railway station: Blackfriars.
NI Part Two.
Real ale.

'Unique' is a much overworked word when it comes to describing pubs. But that's exactly what the Black Friar is. There's nothing else anywhere remotely like its fabulous decorative scheme, either in style or content. But beware – for a really good look it's best to avoid busy weekday lunchtimes and early evenings and try quieter times when you can relax over one of their three or four real ales.

Located on a triangular site opposite Blackfriars station, the pub was built in about 1875 but what makes it so special is a remodelling from about 1905 by the then-publican, Alfred Pettitt, and his architect H Fuller-Clark. Fuller-Clark trained at the Lambeth School of Art and began practice in 1893. His artist was Henry Poole RA.

The theme of the work was the Dominican Friary established here in 1278. The friars – or at least jolly, modern reinvented versions of them – appear everywhere in sculptures, mosaics and metal reliefs. The whole thing is a glorious piece of nonsense but it's carried off with wit and verve.

The most prevalent activities depicted concern the serious matters of eating, drinking and generally enjoying oneself. Hence over the left-hand bar is a scene entitled 'Tomorrow will be Friday' showing fish and eels being collected for the ensuing meatless day. 'Saturday afternoon' sees the friars gardening. Over the magnificent fireplace 'Carols' introduces us to them singing. The most special space, added in 1917-21, is the mosaic-vaulted area under the railway beyond three openings. Lined with marble and alabaster, it has a series of jokey scenes and inscriptions. 'Seize occasion' has a friar boozing; 'Industry is rare' catches one snoozing. Also, don't miss the really marvellous lamp brackets.

Outside there are beautiful metal signs, one of which bears a couple of friars pointing you towards the saloon and helpfully tells you it is nine yards away. Clearly, therefore, the pub had two separate rooms in Mr Pettitt's day and it is not hard to work

Above: **Statue of friar outside the Black Friar**

Below: **Black Friar stained glass window**

RIGHT HAND PAGE >>

Black Friar interior

Above: **Olde Cheshire Cheese exterior**

Middle: **Olde Cheshire Cheese interior signage**

Below: **Wood-panelled corridor inside the Olde Cheshire Cheese**

out where the division would have run. As the two rooms were not originally connected, that no doubt explains why Pettitt and Fuller-Clark felt at liberty to more or less repeat the 'Saturday afternoon' scenes in both areas.

History in the area: The name Blackfriars derives from the Dominican Friars who moved from Holborn to the north bank of the Thames in 1276. The priory remained here until 1538 when it was dissolved by Henry VIII.

OLDE CHESHIRE CHEESE ⑧

145 Fleet Street, Holborn, EC4 2BU
020 7353 6170
Grade II listed.
Tube: Blackfriars.
Railway stations: Blackfriars, City Thameslink.
NI Part Two.
Real ale.
Closed Sunday evenings.

This is a celebrated old establishment in the annals of London pub history but its fame is such that it's best visited at quieter times such as mid-afternoon. It is now owned by Yorkshire brewer, Samuel Smith and serves their one and only real ale. It is hidden away up an alley off Fleet Street and is the result of a post-Great Fire rebuilding in the late 17th century. The frontage in the alley has reconstructed screens which can be rolled up and down to protect the windows. Note the 'fly-screens' behind the windows with the lettering 'OCC'.

What really counts here is the pair of rooms either side of the entrance. The one on the right is a small bar with what might be original panelling from the rebuilding, simple bench seating, a huge fireplace and Victorian counter. Over the entrance is a notice from less egalitarian days, 'Gentlemen only served in this bar'. Under the adjacent glazed screen is similar lettering offering 'Waiter service'. The waiters in question would no doubt have been those servicing the room to the left of the entrance: this is the 'Chop Room', a panelled eating area which recreates the atmosphere of many an eating area in an old tavern. The upper floors are in restaurant use and have panelling of various ages, much of it 20th-century. The pub was extended to the east and a new part added, much of it in about 1992.

History nearby: Fleet Street, the ancient land route between the City and Westminster, recorded as far back as 1002, is named after the River Fleet which (now) flows underground at the bottom of the hill. It is especially associated with newspaper publishing and the first regular daily was produced near its east end in 1702. But it was only in the 19th century that the newspaper industry became dominant over banks, hotels and other offices. The most impressive monument is the Art Deco *Daily Express* building at numbers 120-129. The newspapers vacated the area mostly in the late 1980s.

Above: **Punch Tavern exterior, with Mr Punch sign**
Below: **Painting of Mr Punch**

PUNCH TAVERN ⑨

99 Fleet Street, EC4 1DE
020 7353 6658
Grade II listed.
Tube: Blackfriars.
Railway station: Blackfriars, City Thameslink.
Real ale.
Closed Saturday evenings and Sunday.

A well known institution in lower Fleet Street (but avoid frenetic weekday lunchtimes when you are more or less expected to buy food). It could easily be missed were it not for Mr Punch outside and lavish tiling to the entrance as it lies up a corridor behind a couple of shop fronts. The pub is part of a block built in 1894-7 by architects Saville & Martin and at one time also incorporated the pub round the corner in Bride Lane, the Crown & Sugar Loaf.

The entrance corridor is unlike anything else in a London pub and has extensive tiling, a mosaic floor, mirrors and, either side of the inner doors, large canvas paintings of a very sinister-looking Mr and Mrs Punch (signed by W B Simpson's who were no doubt responsible for the whole decorative scheme).

Inside there has been a good deal of rearrangement and refitting and it is now impossible to work out exactly how things might have been. The fixed seating on the left-hand side seems original and the lovely etched main panels in the bar-back also no doubt date from 1894. But the collection of glass in the lower part of the bar-back has clearly been shuffled. The two skylights in this room add much to its character. The rear room was a bookshop until the 1990s and was brought into use after

PUBLIC HOUSES, INNS, TAVERNS AND ALEHOUSES

One of London's long-lost inns, the once-famous Oxford Arms, Warwick Lane, pictured here in 1856. It was a major coaching centre but was made redundant by the railways. It had galleries on three sides of the courtyard which led to the guest rooms. The fourth side was occupied by stables.
The Builder, 19 April 1856

'Public house' is a term originating in the late 17th century and which embraced a wide variety of establishments for the public consumption of alcohol. The names that described them conveyed very specific meanings although nowadays the distinctions have become completely blurred. 'Inns' were associated with travel, providing accommodation, food and drink for guests and stabling for their horses. They also provided venues for social events, meetings and, often, official functions such as courts. London's coaching

termini had numerous inns of which the great survivor is the George, Southwark (p139). Like other major towns and cities London had its 'taverns'. These had emerged in the 12th and 13th centuries and were places where wine was served. Wine (imported, of course) was expensive and taverns therefore attracted better-off and better-class clients. 'Alehouses' (or 'beerhouses') did exactly what the names imply – they sold ale or beer. They were given a massive boost by the Beer Act of 1830 which allowed any ratepayer to sell beer on payment of an excise fee of just two guineas – 24,342 of them did so across the country before the end of the year and the numbers continued to climb in subsequent years. From 1869 beerhouses were brought back into the main licensing system and their numbers have gradually waned and now they are no more. There were also 'gin-shops' in the early 19th century and 'cider houses', which survived in London in tiny numbers down to the mid-20th century.

The affectionate abbreviation 'pub' is not so very old and seems to emerge in the first half of the 19th century. It only became prevalent in its closing decades and is one of a number of compressed words – like exam, gym and lab – which the Victorians brought into common currency. The early 20th century brought 'roadhouses' catering as 'destination pubs' for the motorised drinker. Pub evolution in the late 20th century has given us 'gastropubs' and 'café bars' whose function and character will be familiar enough to render explanation superfluous. Who knows what another century may bring in terms of new drinking establishments and the names to describe them?

the Punch separated from what is now the Crown & Sugar Loaf. Here the Yorkshire brewer Samuel Smith has recreated a fabulous Victorian-style interior in modern times. They brought the pub back to life in June 2004 with a stunning display of etched and cut mirrors, carved woodwork, a marble counter and lovely mosaic floor. The decorated ceiling is the only original Victorian feature but no matter – the whole thing is done with such fantastic panache.

TIPPERARY ⑩

66 Fleet Street, Holborn, EC4 1HT
020 7583 6470
Grade II listed.
Tube: Blackfriars.
Railway stations: Blackfriars,
City Thameslink.
Real ale.
Closed Sat and Sun from 6pm.

Claimed as London's first Irish pub, the Tipperary was taken over by Mooney's of Dublin in 1895 who promptly refitted this small establishment under architect R L Cox. You will spot the Mooney's lettering at the front doorstep and the shamrock-embellished mosaic running down the right-hand side floor in an attempt to establish the Irish credentials. Today the pub is part of the Greene King empire and serves their usual ales. However, some Irishness lives on with plenty of Guinness sold, a big thing being made of St Patrick's Day and, of course, the survival of Mooney's late-Victorian interior.

On the ground floor there is a single, long bar stretching away from the street that was once lined with boozy newspaper reporters. It's fully panelled on the right-hand side, has a servery on the left with a carved bar-back and has a pair of magnificent glass panels advertising stout and whisky. They are signed 'H West, Houghton Street, Strand, WC'. Given that it's the Irish spirit that is promoted you may be surprised by the spelling. We think of Scottish *whisky* but Irish *whiskey* but there was no such convention until well into the 20th century – hence we get Jameson's 'whisky' here. The upstairs bar is known as the Boar's Head Bar after the original name of the pub – it only acquired its present title after 1918 to commemorate the Great War song.

WEST

W1 to W14

ARGYLL ARMS ❶

18 Argyll Street, Soho, W1F 7TP
020 7734 6117.
Grade II* listed.
Tube: Oxford Circus.
NI Part One.
Real ale.

MAP: W1

The Argyll is an astonishing survival and a welcome escape from frenetic Oxford Street with food and a good range of real ales available. It has one of the most important late Victorian interiors in London and, like the Prince Alfred (p55), shows how pub proprietors and their clients liked small, cosy drinking spaces. However, whereas the Prince Alfred has a peninsula-style servery with radiating screens, the Argyll has a long, straight servery and a series of screened-off drinking areas sandwiched between it and the corridor.

The building dates from 1868 but the fittings are from an 1890s remodelling undertaken for the proprietor E Bratt (the architect was probably Robert Sawyer). At the front there are two entrances, the right-hand one leading into a drinking area while on the left a corridor leads to the rear of the building. The mirrors on the left-hand wall enhance the sumptuous atmosphere with reflections of the screens and glass opposite and light from the lamps.

At the back the 'saloon and dining room' cut into a high-level glass panel announces this as the smartest part of the pub where there is another glittering display of mirrors. A magnificent, swirly iron stair rail leads to the now modernised first floor. Other features to relish are the highly decorated ceiling, probably dating from 1868; an immensely deep, decorated cornice in the rear parts; an ornamented column in the back area and a delightful little glazed-in office within the servery.

History in the street: Argyll Street was laid out by John Campbell, the second Duke of Argyll, one of the Duke of Marlborough's leading generals. It was in the heart of fashionable London

<< *LEFT HAND PAGE*
Mirrored corridor in the Argyll Arms

Below: **Argyll Arms exterior**

and the Campbells built their London residence, Argyll House, on the opposite side of the road between 1735 and 1750. The London Palladium, by the great theatre architect Frank Matcham, was built in 1909-10.

COACH & HORSES ❷

29 Greek Street, Soho, W1D 5DH
020 7437 5920
Grade II listed.
Tube: Leicester Square; Tottenham Court Road.
Real ale.

Above: **Curved corner of the Coach & Horses**
Below: **Coach & Horses interior**

Much-loved by its regulars this pub (sometimes known as 'Norman's') has a most unusual appearance with its rows of detached cast-iron columns on both street façades supporting the upper floors. It was completely remodelled early in the post-war period (although just possibly the 1930s) and this work survives largely intact. The pub is divided into three spaces by a pair of screens. These have now lost their double doors and so the character of the interior has changed substantially. But the wall panelling, tapering bar counter, bar-back and (in two areas) spittoon troughs all survive. Two blocks of the troughs have ring-pulls that are unique to this pub. A contemporary dumb waiter and fireplace are situated in the right-hand area of the pub.

Nearby: The St James's Tavern, 45 Great Windmill Street, is worth a visit for its late Victorian tiled panels. The main series of four depict Shakespearian scenes (conveniently labelled) and are a good example of a form of decoration popular in more up-market pubs in around 1900.

History in the area: This part of Soho has been part of London's literary and entertainment scene for centuries. One of its most famous residents latterly was the late Jeffrey Bernard (1932-1997) who wrote for the *New Statesman* and later *The Spectator*. He frequented the Coach and Horses and in the play *Jeffrey Bernard is Unwell* by Keith Waterhouse, the actor Peter O'Toole played the part of Bernard issuing a monologue in the pub, which was recreated on stage. The long-serving landlord, Norman Balon, who retired in May 2006, also became famous as the self-proclaimed 'London's rudest landlord' and author of his agreeably entitled memoirs, *You're Barred, You Bastards.*

DOG & DUCK ❸

18 Bateman Street, Soho, W1D 3AJ
020 7494 0697
Grade II listed.
Tube: Tottenham Court Road.
NI Part Two.
Real ale.

A gorgeous, small and very popular (i.e. packed) Soho pub, it was built in 1897 to designs by the architect Francis Chambers. The exterior has glazed brick upper floors incorporating a stone carving of the animals mentioned in its name (note also the delightful mosaic of the animals at the Frith Street entrance). The ground floor has polished granite and larvikite facings, which probably date from a 1930s makeover.

The interior is also a mixture of Victorian and inter-war work – the former represented by extensive wall-tiling and a couple of large, framed advertising mirrors promoting long-vanished tobacco and mineral water products. The more restrained work of around 1930 is found in the woodwork of the left-hand part. This was also probably the time when the pub was opened up and took its present single-space layout. Its Victorian predecessor would undoubtedly have had several divisions but it is hard to work out exactly how things were. The present servery now blocks a former outside door.

History in the area: In the 16th century Soho, was Henry VIII's hunting ground. In the following century the area was home to religious refugees including Huguenots who took over a chapel in Hog Lane (later Crown Street). Nowadays the site is covered by St Martin's School of Art, Charing Cross Road.

Above: **Façade of the Dog & Duck**
Below: **Tiled Dog & Duck interior**

FRENCH HOUSE (formerly York Minster) ❹

49 Dean Street, Soho, W1D 5BE
020 7437 2799
Grade II listed.
Tube: Leicester Square.

This tiny single-room pub in the heart of Soho is a real institution with a long and strong French connection. It also has a good restaurant upstairs. It was taken over by the Francophone Belgian Victor Berlemont in 1914 (see framed cuttings and pictures in

Above: **1930s interior of the French House**

Below: **French House façade with its famous French and British flags**

Below: **Grand exterior of the George**

the bar) when it was called the York Minster, although by the 1920s it had acquired the nickname 'the French Pub'. It was rebuilt in 1937 to designs of architect Alfred W Blomfield.

Later, there was some wartime bomb damage and partial refitting afterwards which created the pub we see today. The present name appeared in 1981 to celebrate the French ties. The fittings in the small, single bar are all very much of a piece with narrow, elongated panels featuring in the wall panelling, a counter (with doors for access to the beer engines in former days), and sash windows. There is a dumb waiter in the middle of the bar-back. As might be expected wine easily outsells beer. Breton cider is popular and it is claimed that more Ricard is shifted here than at any other UK outlet.

History on the spot: During the World War II this pub was a focus for the Free French and, it is claimed, General de Gaulle was one of its illustrious patrons. In 1949, in his delightful book about London pubs, Maurice Gorham noted 'a wall-full of photographs of French boxers and cyclists, and French spoken freely on both sides of the bar'.

GEORGE Ⓢ

55 Great Portland Street, Fitzrovia, W1W 7LQ
020 7636 0863
Not listed
Tube: Oxford Circus.
Real ale.

This is a popular pub, owned by Greene King, in the heart of Fitzrovia sitting proudly and ornately on the corner of two streets. It has now been turned into a single drinking space, yet it is still well worth a visit for its collection of surviving, excellent late-Victorian fixtures and fittings.

The panelled bar counter seems original and behind it is a magnificent five-bay back-fitting with etched and gilded mirrors with the sprays of flowers and foliage that were so popular with pub fitters of the day. Yet, without doubt, the most appealing part of the pub is the left-hand side with its wood-panelled walls, more etched and gilded mirrors, and delightful ceramic panels. In the front area are three elongated panels of ladies and gents on horseback. The rear area has the air of a gentleman's club, fully panelled to the ceiling and decorated with mirrors and tiles with beautifully realised painted hunting dogs and a stag – the pub's patrons probably aspired to such a way of life.

History in the area: The name Fitzrovia, believed to have been coined in the 20th century, derives from the name of the man who became Lord Southampton, the Hon Charles Fitzroy. He developed the area in the 18th century with Fitzroy Square its splendid focus. In the 1930s and 1940s Fitzrovia was the haunt of artists and writers, some of them working for the BBC. Among the latter was Julian Maclaren-Ross who sometimes frequented the George and immortalised the atmosphere of the area in his *Memoirs of the Forties*.

GUINEA ⑥

30 Bruton Place, Mayfair, W1J 6NL
020 7409 1728
Not listed.
Tube: Bond Street.
Real ale.

Above: **Front bar and its screen at the Guinea**
Below: **Crowd of drinkers outside the Guinea**

In a back street in the heart of Mayfair, this Young's pub occupies a three-storey brick building with a prominent oriel window. The front windows have etched glass bearing the name of the pub and the highly suspect intelligence that it was 'established 1423' (when Mayfair was little more than ploughed fields). Its chief interest lies in the evidence of the way Victorian pubs were subdivided. On the left the door glass identifies a 'private bar' while that on the right mentions a 'lounge bar'. And inside there is the very rare survival of a screen on the left-hand side which still retains its door. Screens like this were once absolutely standard equipment in thousands of London pubs.

The right-hand side would have had a screen between the front and rear areas (note how the ceiling differs: boarded at the front, plain plaster at the rear). The Victorian bar counter, with panelling and console brackets, remains as do parts of the barback. The restaurant area at the back left has old panelling and has probably long been a pub room.

History in the area: The affluent area of Mayfair is owned by several landlords including the Grosvenor family and the Crown. It was named after an annual fair held in May. Bruton Place itself housed stables and coach houses for the wealthy residents of Berkeley Square and Bruton Street.

Above: **Inn 1888 with its decorative windows**

RIGHT HAND PAGE >>
Beautiful tiles and mirrors inside Inn 1888

Above: **Stags Head, interior**
Below: **Stags Head, exterior detail**

INN 1888 (formerly Devonshire Arms) ⑦

21a Devonshire Street, Marylebone, W1G 6PD
020 7935 8327
Not listed.
Tube: Baker Street, Regent's Park.
Real ale.

Now a smart, small, single-bar pub, the great feature here is the tiling and mirror work lining the inside walls. As the present name helpfully implies, this red-brick building dates back to 1888: the ground floor has a larvikite plinth and red granite pilasters. The other feature that can be spotted outside is the pretty stained and painted glass borders to the lower parts of the windows which include representations of Michaelmas daisies. In the heads of the windows you can also make out delicate filigree piercing.

The tiled walls have a yellow ochre-coloured dado, above which is an early type of Art Nouveau frieze, and, then, on the upper part of the walls, a series of panels divided by wooden pilasters. Each panel has an ornamented mirror set within a wooden frame. The colouration of this upper tiling is unique and is a warm mixture of beige, buff and red. Near the side entrance is a splendid advertising mirror promoting the wares of Pocock & Pearce of Pancras Road who tell us they are the sole proprietors of Paddy Liqueur Irish Whisky and 'The Nurse's' brand of bottled beers. There is a little vignette in the centre of 'Paddy and Polly' cavorting about, seemingly drunk.

STAG'S HEAD ⑧

102 New Cavendish Street, Fitzrovia, W1W 6XW
020 7580 8313
Not listed.
Tube: Great Portland Street, Regent's Park.
Real ale.

In complete contrast to late Victorian ornateness, this corner-site pub is a rare example of late 1930s sleek streamlining. The builders were the Scottish brewer William Younger who had previously gone for a nostalgic, half-timbered style for their pubs dotted over central London. No more fancy foliage or gritty materials, just a smooth brick building with a rounded

corner and metal windows. Note the metal door (left) and curving glass to the right-hand entrance.

The interior is a single space with a servery with panelled bar counter along the rear wall. In contrast to the exterior, there is little sense of modernity here because the extensive wall panelling does hark back to the ever-popular Tudor revival. Younger's seem to have been setting out their stall to cater for stand-up drinking by workers from the surrounding offices – hence the peninsula-style projections to prop up customers and their drinks. All in all, this pub is a rather special survivor.

History nearby: In May 1932 the British Broadcasting Corporation moved from Savoy Hill off the Strand to their brand new Portland stone building, Broadcasting House, Portland Place. The main entrance in Langham Place has bronze doors and a beautiful bas-relief by Eric Gill depicting Prospero and Ariel – the building is a real architectural gem.

Above: **Inside the Tottenham, all mirrors and mahogany panelling**
Below: **Tottenham frontage – the last pub remaining on Oxford Street**

TOTTENHAM 🄊

6 Oxford Street, Fitzrovia, W1D 1AN
020 7636 7201
Grade II listed.
Tube: Tottenham Court Road.
NI Part Two.
Real ale.

Right by Tottenham Court Road tube station, this is the last-remaining pub on the whole length of Oxford Street and is busy morning, noon and night. It was built in 1892 in a Flemish Renaissance style to the designs of architects Saville & Martin and occupies a narrow plot which no doubt reflects a long history.

The pub now consists of a long, single space, which is the result of the amalgamation of at least two rooms from the original Victorian pub. There is a good deal of decoration to admire here, especially in the rear part where there is a tiled frieze with swirling foliage, an ornate mahogany-surround fireplace, mirror and mahogany panelling, and a skylight (which unfortunately has been ruined by unbelievably inappropriate modern coloured glass). Down the right-hand wall is a series of mirrors and paintings, which depict three of the four seasons (number four has been lost at some stage). On the ceiling throughout the pub is a series of painted roundels of Classical subjects.

MITRE ⑩

24 Craven Terrace, Bayswater, W2 3QH
020 7262 5240.
Grade II listed.
Tube: Lancaster Gate.
Real ale.

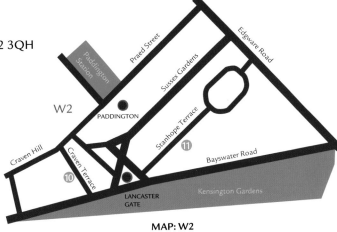

MAP: W2

Despite much wall and screen removal, there is still much of interest to see here, especially in the fine glasswork. The Mitre occupies a triangular corner site and has an unusual pair of slightly curved doors at the angle, leading to an attractive little lobby where the pub name appears on the inner door. Before going in, the windows are worth a look for the unusual ironwork in the uprights and sub-Gothic tracery. Very sadly the glass has been replaced with plain sheets.

The most impressive work is on the right-hand side with mosaic flooring at the entrance, which stretches back into two more panels. In this area is an excellent display of etched, cut and orange-coloured glass, including a door panel advertising the 'ladies bar'. This shows how some pubs at the end of the 19th century were starting to provide a secure environment for respectable women who previously would have regarded the pub as completely out of bounds. Other glass advertises a billiard room (which seems to have been upstairs) and a saloon, which has a small skylight.

Above: **Etched glass in the Mitre**

Below: **Mitre mosaic floor**

VICTORIA ⑪

10a Strathearn Place, Bayswater, W2 2NH
020 7724 1191
Grade II listed.
Tube: Lancaster Gate, Paddington.
Railway station: Paddington.
NI Part Two.
Real ale.

Between Paddington Station and Hyde Park, this Fuller's-owned corner-site pub has some very early and spectacular fittings. Such was the amount of pub renovation at the end of the 19th century and since, that any fittings before the late-Victorian

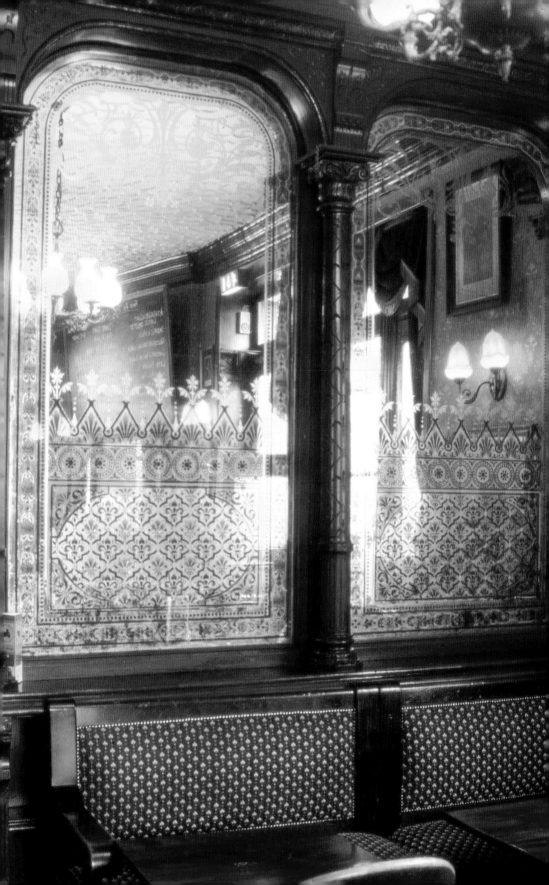

era are incredibly rare. Those at the Victoria are stylistically mid-Victorian and a precise date – 1864 – is suggested by the date on a clock in the bar-back fitting. This, and a side wall, have large mirrors with intricate gilding and coloured decoration, each panel being separated from the others by detached columns with lozenge and fleur-de-lys decoration.

In the angle of the building is a delicate Regency-style fireplace containing a print of Queen Victoria, Prince Albert and their numerous progeny. The counter is a piece from 1864 with panelled bays divided by fluted pilasters. It still retains a brass water-dispenser for diluting spirits – still fully functioning. Mounted on the long wall are coloured prints of soldiers in wooden frames but these are most probably a relatively modern (though now smoke-stained) addition. There are several outside doors and these would have led originally to a series of internal drinking areas, separated by screenwork. Upstairs the Theatre Bar has ornate fittings imported from the Gaiety Theatre in about 1958.

Above: **Rounded, stucco exterior of the Victoria**

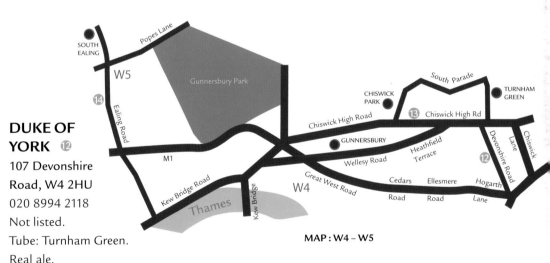

MAP : W4 – W5

DUKE OF YORK ⑫

107 Devonshire Road, W4 2HU
020 8994 2118
Not listed.
Tube: Turnham Green.
Real ale.

An attractive corner-site local of 1926 designed by T H Nowell Parr who built a number of distinguished pubs in west London. The three original rooms are still very much in evidence. The one on the corner entrance was probably the public bar, which has now been linked to the two beyond. The first two rooms have bar counters with simple but elegant panelling. As in his other pubs Parr aimed to create a sense of comfortable 'olde

<< *LEFT HAND PAGE*

Original gilded Victorian mirrors in the Victoria

Above: **Duke of York interior**

worldiness' with wall panelling rising to slightly over half the height of the walls, and exposed ceiling beams in all rooms.

In the 'public bar' there is now a series of screens running out from the outside wall and creating intimate small drinking areas. These are modern but seem to have had Victorian glass panels incorporated into them.

Nearby: Just down the road on the opposite side is another Parr pub, the Devonshire House, where the red brick detailing is the same as at the Duke of York.

You may also care to seek out the Tabard, 2 Bath Road, W4, built in 1880 by the great architect Norman Shaw as the pub for the new, refined garden suburb of Bedford Park. Although very substantially refitted the beautiful William De Morgan wall tiles survive. The counter seems original but the bar-back and seating in the rear, lower area are good modern work in an Arts and Crafts style. The right-hand bar has obviously lost a partition (hence the two entrance doors).

Above: **Ornate Edwardian counter and bar-back, Old Pack Horse**
Below: **Old Pack Horse exterior**

OLD PACK HORSE

434 Chiswick High Road, London, W4 5TF
020 8994 2872
Grade II listed.
Tube: Chiswick Park.
Real ale.

An architectural extravaganza of 1910 to designs by the prolific T H Nowell Parr for Fuller, Smith & Turner who still own it (it also doubles as a Thai restaurant). The Edwardian free-style exterior has abundant faïence on the ground floor and lots of most interesting detailing in the floors above. Three original rooms are still clearly discernible and retain their names in the etched window glass (some of it gently curved).

Easily the best space is the saloon (on Acton Lane) with its panelling and delightful alcove and original fireplace, which sits behind a Tudor arch. Such arches are a Parr favourite (as elsewhere in this pub). The counter in the saloon is original too and has highly unusual detailing, while the surround of the bar-back is original although the centre part is, unfortunately, modern work. Round the corner the main bar-back, however, is original as is the main run of the counter. The counter in the area on the corner of the pub is a crude cobbling together of old and new

NOWELL PARR, A FINE PUB ARCHITECT

Thomas Henry Nowell Parr (1864-1933) has more pubs to his credit in this book than any other architect. There are six of them, all in West London and dating from the early years of the 20th century. He was one of those who turned his back on the florid extravaganzas of late-Victorian pub building and provided his clients with something that relied more on line and proportion than showy decoration.

Nowell Parr was born in Handsworth, now part of Birmingham, in 1864, served his articles with the Birmingham firm of Dunn & Hipkiss and became an assistant in Walsall Corporation Architects' Department from 1890 to 1894. From here he moved to Middlesex to work in Brentford Urban District Council Architects' Department. From 1897 to 1907 he was Architect, Engineer and Surveyor to Brentford UDC and, while retaining this post, set up his own architectural practice in about 1900. Among his designs for the local authority is the library, begun in 1903 and opened on 9 May 1904 by the American millionaire philanthropist, Andrew Carnegie, who had donated £5,000 towards the cost.

The same year (1904) a Boatmen's Institute was built for the London City Mission to Parr's design on the Grand Union Canal at Brentford – it is now a private house.

In 1914 Parr moved from 42 Cranley Gardens, South Kensington to 52 Kew Bridge Road, Brentford, which is very near the Express Tavern (p76). In 1925 he became a Fellow of the Royal Institute of British Architects. He died on 23 September 1933. At some point his son, John Nowell (died 1975), joined the practice, hence it became known as Nowell Parr & Son.

Trademark features in his pubs include Tudor arches, plain but very stylish woodwork, delicate coloured glass motifs, and applied wooden beams on ceilings. The pubs mentioned in this book are as follows: the Duke of York (p45) and the Old Pack Horse (p46), both in Chiswick, for Fuller's; the Forester, West Ealing (p67), and the Three Horseshoes, Southall (p78), for the Royal Brewery, Brentford; also the Devonshire House, Chiswick, W4 (p46) under the Duke of York), and the Duke of Kent, West Ealing (p64).

elements. All the rooms in the pub have another Parr characteristic – exposed wooden studding and beams. Don't miss the stained glass packhorses and Fuller's griffin. Throughout the pub there are very attractive chairs with elongated lozenges in the backs, which perhaps date from 1910. One of the redundant doorways in the pub must have served as an off-sales.

History nearby: Round the corner to the north is Charles Holden's Chiswick Park underground station of 1931-2 with its wonderful Art Deco semi-circular ticket hall.

Top: **Ealing Park Tavern, Edwardian interior tiling and glass**

Above: **Plaque inside the Dove showing the height of a flood in 1928**

Right: **Dove sign**

EALING PARK TAVERN

222 South Ealing Road, Ealing, W5 4RL
020 8758 1879.
Not listed.
Tube: Northfields, South Ealing.
Real ale.

An epic piece of Edwardian pub architecture, it forms a real landmark on the west side of South Ealing Road. In recent times it has taken on a gastro-pub orientation but drinkers are still welcome and they are rewarded by various real ales and considerable remains from the original building.

A tour might start outside with the highly impressive recessed porch framed by a timber arch with bulgy columns and the monogram of the founders, the Royal Brewery (Brentford) Ltd, which ceased production in 1923. This porch has lovely green tiling and Art Nouveau-style lettering advertising the saloon, which is also named on the brass door plate.

The main drinking bar fronts Carlyle Road and has a long bar counter with a raked front. The lettering on the bar-back fitting tells us this was once a Courage house (in the days when brewers still owned pubs!). Behind comes a room with two-thirds-height panelling. On the right of the main entrance is a lovely room with still more wall panelling and an intriguingly shaped bar counter.

Above: **Ealing Park Tavern exterior**
Below: **Long bar counter inside the Ealing Park Tavern**

DOVE

19 Upper Mall, Hammersmith, W6 9TA
020 8748 9474
Grade II listed.
Tube: Ravenscourt Park.
Real ale.

Celebrated far and wide, the Fuller's-owned Dove overlooks the Thames and is approached by a narrow alley from the river. It was probably built in the early to mid-18th century and then refronted in the 19th. Its amazingly tiny snug, with match-boarded counter and fixed wall benches, is claimed by *Guinness World Records* to be the smallest public bar in Britain. However, research by beer writer Martyn Cornell suggests it

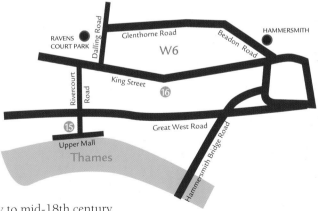

MAP : W6

Above: **Dove interior, parts of which may date from the 18th century**

may not be as old as one might think. He believes it was installed some time after 1911 by the then licensee who thought his single-room, fully licensed premises contravened the Licensing Consolidation Act of 1910 and so he created the diminutive snug to rectify matters. However, he needn't have bothered, Cornell argues, since, if a single-room, fully licensed house had existed before 1872 (as was the case with the Dove), the Act did not make it a necessity to put in a second room. However, had you been drinking here on 7 January 1928 you'd have been waist-high in water judging by a small brass plaque recording that day's mighty inundation.

The other front room is historic too in terms of its wall seating and counter. Some of the woodwork here, along with that in the vestibule, might even go back to the 18th century and, if so, could be some of the earliest purpose-built pub fittings around. Post-war repairs in 1948 saw the addition of the substantial brick fireplace with its exuberant Portland stone carving of the dove returning to Noah's Ark with an olive branch. The rear room at the Dove is modern but the terrace beyond overlooking the Thames is a delightful place to enjoy a drink on a fine day.

History nearby: Kelmscott House, 26 Upper Mall, was named as such by the artist and designer William Morris who rented it from its owner, the poet and novelist George MacDonald. Morris established his printing and design works here.

HOPE & ANCHOR ⑯

20 Macbeth Street, Hammersmith, W6 9JJ
020 8748 1873
Grade II listed.
Tube: Hammersmith, Ravenscourt Park.
NI Part One

Below: **Hope & Anchor sign**

This drinkers' local is a very good example of a largely unaltered, modest Truman's pub of about 1930. Planned as part of a housing development, it retains its separate public bar and saloon. The former is the larger but in terms of fittings there is little to differentiate them. Both have wall panelling and fixed seats and the counters are the same plain, panelled design while both bar-backs each have an Art Deco clock.

Many pubs had spittoon troughs in front of bar counters and that in the saloon bar here is an excellent example. This trough has timber edging and is lined with brown and white chequered tiles. There's even a small opening at the counter corner to sweep the bits and pieces together. Other original features are the brick fireplaces and, in the saloon, typical Truman's lettering on the panelling advertising their wares. There is original tiling in the saloon bar.

The one big change is the loss of the off-sales compartment – traceable in the closed doorway on the (puzzlingly named) Riverside Gardens side and the stopped-off spittoon trough. There is a pleasant garden area beyond a loggia outside the saloon bar.

History opposite: Across Macbeth Street is one of London's Board Schools (1896) built in the late 19th century to educate children in architecturally uplifting surroundings.

Above: **King's Arms interior**

KING'S ARMS

110 Uxbridge Road, Hanwell, W7 3SU
020 8567 2370
Not listed.
Railway station: Hanwell.
NI Part One.
Real ale.

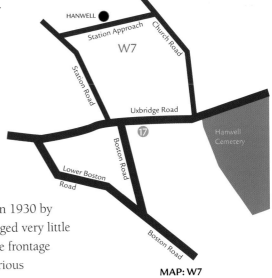

MAP: W7

This large but basic high street pub was rebuilt in 1930 by brewers Mann, Crossman & Paulin and has changed very little in the intervening three-quarters of a century. The frontage is quite plain and has doors which lead to the various separate rooms inside.

On either side there are two rooms, one behind the other and in between them, at the front, a small private bar. On the left the public bar has what is now a games room behind it: the only real change is the loss of double doors between the two. The same layout (and loss of doors) is found on the right but the hierarchical distinction between the two sides is reflected in the greater elaboration of the counter on the saloon side, which is also graced with wall panelling. In the middle of the servery is an example of a publican's private office. The toilets at the back on the left-hand side still retain their original tiling.

On the far right externally is a staircase leading to an upstairs function room and further right still is the residue of what was originally an off-sales shop.

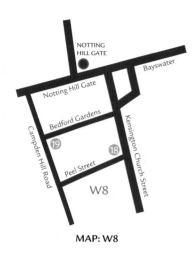

MAP: W8

Above: **Churchill Arms exterior**

Below: **Pub paraphernalia over the bar, Churchill Arms**

CHURCHILL ARMS ⑱

119 Kensington Church Street, Kensington, W8 7LN
020 7727 4242
Not listed.
Tube: Notting Hill Gate.
Real ale.

A popular Fuller's pub, which is often very busy as much of its clientele is attracted by the excellent Thai food. It was built in the Victorian era but given a complete internal refit between the wars. There would have been separate rooms, of course, at that time but all the partitions have gone leaving a U-shaped drinking area. But most of the rest of the c.1930 work survives.

The windows are very attractive with their canted bays and charming stained glass details. Then there is the bar counter, most of which has panels with triple mouldings round it, though the smaller, right-hand counter is much plainer. This makes it clear that the bars must have been separated by a partition and, if you look closely, you can see in the window-sill a small piece of patching where the old screen stood.

The walls are extensively panelled and there are a couple of pretty tiled fireplaces. There are also two sets of snob-screens mounted on the counter: what age they are is a moot point. When the present licensee came in the mid-1980s they formed a continuous run but it's hard to believe such an intrusive feature would have been put in during the 1930s when people favoured unencumbered counters. It's likely they were a later restoration.

WINDSOR CASTLE ⑲

114 Campden Hill Road, Kensington, W8 7AR
020 7243 9551
Not listed.
Tube: Notting Hill Gate.
NI Part One.
Real ale.

A well known pub in this affluent neighbourhood, the Windsor Castle is an interesting illustration of the survival of Victorian-type drinking arrangements right up to the 1930s. This plain, two-storey building of around 1825 sits at the summit of Campden Hill Road and was refitted in around 1933. We know this because in the 'Sherry Bar' there is a plaque explaining that the oak used in that room was felled in the period 1930-32. Also helpful is the fact that the door glass names each of the three traditional rooms. The Sherry Bar is entered off Peel Street, the private bar is on the corner, while the Campden Bar lies along Campden Hill Road. The mahogany bar-back is the sole survivor from the Victorian era. Otherwise the fittings are pretty much intact from the 1930s, even down to some pretty Arts and Crafts door furniture. Pride of place goes to the two screens which create three rooms very much in the manner of a Victorian public house. There are even low service doors to give access to pot boys and cleaning staff. All the rooms have attractive fixed seating which looks as though it could have come from an ancient country pub. The private bar and Campden Bar have counters with raked matchboard panelling whereas the Sherry Bar has fielded panelling. The latter also has a brick fireplace and, over it, a much yellowed picture of the castle from which the pub takes its name – supposedly because of the fact that on a clear day Windsor Castle could be seen from it.

History in the area: Campden Hill Road takes its name from Campden House, the residence of Viscount Campden which was demolished in about 1900. In the 19th and early 20th century many writers, including H G Wells and Henry James, used to meet in number 80 Campden Hill Road, and the novelist John Galsworthy lived at number 82.

Above: **Windsor Castle exterior**

Below: **Intact 1930s interior of the Windsor Castle**

CHIPPENHAM ㉑

207 Shirland Road, Maida Vale, W9 2EX
020 7624 2270
Not listed.
Tube: Maida Vale.

A shadow of its original Victorian self, and now as much a cheap B&B as a pub, the reason to visit is the tile and mirror decoration. The right-hand entrance is the best place to start. Late Victorian ironwork bearing the name of the pub fills the head of the arch to a small lobby. This has a mosaic floor and full-height tiling and a mirror on the right-hand side. The tall bluish and beige panels have trails of what

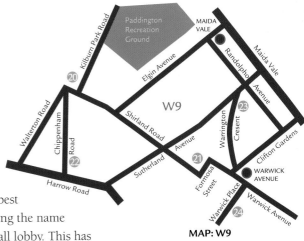

MAP: W9

are perhaps meant to be stylised pomegranates. The contractor who put all this together used the opportunity for a little self-promotion, signing the mirror 'J Higgs, Builder and Fitter, Upper Park Place NW'.

Mr Higgs continued his scheme inside with more tall 'pomegranate' panels and plain mirrors down the walls of a large, long room that stretches out behind. At the rear, in a shallow alcove, the decoration changes to stylised flowers set against a plain, brown tiled ground. On the left-hand side of the pub is a very different tile scheme with the main motif being blue and off-white panels of swirling Arabesque foliage and pairs of birds. The bar counter is Victorian but otherwise the pub has been opened up and modernised. It still operates as a pub-cum-hotel.

PRINCE ALFRED ㉑

5a Formosa Street, Maida Vale, W9 1EE
020 7286 3287
Grade II listed.
Tube: Warwick Avenue.
NI Part Two.
Real ale.

Above: **Chippenham exterior**
Below: **Chippenham 'pomegranates'**

<< LEFT HAND PAGE
Prince Alfreds interior

Below: **Prince Alfreds tiled entrance**

Outside, the Prince is nothing terribly exciting – a three-storey Italianate building in keeping with its surroundings – but inside shows to perfection how late Victorian drinkers liked their pubs. The building went up in about 1865 but was given a complete refit around 1898. From outside look carefully at the exposed ceiling on the ground floor and you can see how timber and glass screenwork has been inserted, cutting across the patterned decoration. Also note the tiles and mosaic in the entrance.

The interior has the only peninsula-style servery to retain all of its original surrounding drinking areas – no fewer than five of them, each with its own external entrance. They are separated by timber and glass screens, all of them with a low service door for the use of, say, pot boys and cleaners. The smallest compartment has a set of snob screens – swivelling glazed panels, which gave posh patrons a sense of separation from the serving staff. In the middle of the servery is a wonderfully tall, carved fitment, which is secured to the ceiling by ironwork. All this late Victorian work gives the pub a delicate Rococo feel. The pub underwent a refurbishment in 2001 to turn it into a dining pub.

THE GOLDEN AGE OF LONDON PUB-BUILDING

When thinking about pub heritage, most of us are likely to call to mind the splendours of the late Victorian age. 'Gin palaces' we often call them for short although, strictly, that term is incorrect because true gin palaces were a feature of the earlier 19th century and were dedicated largely to the consumption (often in great quantities) of gin, spirits and fortified wines. But the name stuck for the kind of elaborate, highly decorated pubs that were fitted out in grand style in the last couple of decades of the century. Unlike today's throw-away pub-fitting culture, the Victorians built to last and, where it has been allowed to, their work

*Temperance campaign postcard advocating water to drink instead of alchohol. **Andrew Davis collection***

lives on. So much was done at the time that it survives in some quantity. Far from despising them as old-fashioned, today's generation of pubgoers crowd into establishments such as the Princess Louise, Holborn (p13), or the Warrington, Maida Vale (p58), precisely because they are magnificent places to go for a drink in opulent historic surroundings.

Why was there such a phenomenal amount of work going on in London pubs at this time? The reasons are several and intertwined. First of all there was a strong move by respectable Victorian society to get pubs to clean up their act. They were often perceived as dens of iniquity, drunkenness and vice and mainly patronised by working class people who were themselves in much need of personal improvement. In this the role of the temperance movement was crucial. Now largely forgotten, temperance (and total abstinence) campaigners exerted increasing influence from the 1830s and by the late 19th century held considerable political clout via their allies in the Liberal party. There was great pressure, including support from licensing magistrates, to improve the quality and respectability of the public house.

The pub also had to compete as never before. In early Victorian London working class and lower middle-class people (the main patrons of the pub) had few recreational opportunities beyond it. By the 1890s it was a very different story. In what was by then the world's wealthiest country people had ample

The Island Queen, Islington, one of many pubs sumptuously refitted at the end of the 19th century (p101)

For Victorian drinkers etched windows and doors formed a semi-secretive veil between the enticing world of the pub and the, often, harsh reality that lay outside it: these are at the Boleyn, East Ham (p122)

possibilities for spending their unprecedented disposable income and increased leisure time – football matches and other sporting events, excursions, music hall, clubs, educational institutes, even for many an annual holiday by the sea, and, shortly, the cinema to name but a few. Pubs had to make more effort to pull in the customers and they did so with gusto.

Also there was a steady reduction in the number of pubs from 1870 due to a concerted campaign by magistrates to suppress the most badly-managed beerhouses and to limit the number of fully licensed premises. Yet at the same time the population was rising, thus, potentially, making each pub a more valuable asset. Entrepreneurs therefore saw suitably appointed and improved pubs as valuable commercial opportunities and some of them busily developed what we would describe today as pub chains. So did the brewers. They either bought up numerous premises or loaned money to those who agreed to take their beer. This latter occurrence became such a particular feature of the London pub trade that over time it became known as the 'London system'. In 1895 the Conservatives, who did not share the anti-drink stance of

the Liberals, came to power, and the drink trade felt it could look forward to a few years of security. Everything at this time conspired to create a mass of public house speculation and rising prices for the pubs themselves. The Chippenham, Maida Vale (p53), which had cost just £17,500 in 1880 changed hands for a phenomenal £95,000 in 1896, possibly the second highest price paid for a pub at the height of this boom. Such valuable assets also needed to be suitably appointed both without and within.

But, as ever, after the boom came the bust. The price of pubs collapsed and there were many bankruptcies from 1899 among those who had spent freely in the expectation of an ever-rising market. Consequently we find relatively few pubs built in London in the Edwardian years, which, in any case, were a time of general economic sluggishness. Building starts again falteringly on the eve of the Great War, examples in this book being the Forester, West Ealing (p67) and the Lord Clyde, Borough (p140).

The Forester, Ealing, of 1909 shows how the Edwardians tended to use a far more restrained decorative style than the Victorians (p67)

Above: **Angled exterior, the Skiddaw**

RIGHT HAND PAGE >>

Top: **Skiddaw interior with distinctive mosaic floor**

Bottom: **The Warrington's opulent interior.** *Photo: Ben Anders*

SKIDDAW ㉒

46 Chippenham Road, Maida Hill, W9 2AF
020 7432 4340
Not listed.
Tube: Westbourne Park.
Real ale.

This is a prominent corner-site Victorian pub which underwent a major refurbishment in 2005. This transformed it into an establishment which has earned it an enviable reputation for eating and drinking yet at the same time many of the historic features have been preserved. The central serving area remains, albeit with changes for food service, and therefore the Victorian counter survives.

On the left-hand side (approached from the Chippenham Road entrance) there are some impressive reminders from Victorian days. The mosaic floor announces the name of the pub and there are some mirror and floral tile strips on the left-hand wall. Also, the glass in two of the doors names the saloon bar that lay beyond. Here there is some very fine mahogany wall panelling and also three stained glass panels but these have no doubt been resited. The main panel is of a girl playing a lyre. Sadly this is not glass painting at its best and reflects the cheaper, popular end of the market at the end of the 19th century.

Below: **Marble fireplace, the Warrington.** *Photo: Ben Anders*

WARRINGTON ㉓

93 Warrington Crescent, Maida Vale, W9 1EH
020 7592 7960
Grade II listed.
Tube: Maida Vale, Warwick Avenue.
NI Part Two
Real ale.

Part of celebrity chef Gordon Ramsay's small but growing pub chain, this is a spacious, stucco-fronted hotel put up in the middle of the 19th century. It was given a major update later in the century, probably in the 1890s, and the glorious tiled columns to the entrance porch and a huge mosaic floor bearing the name of the pub give some idea of the richness that lies on the other side of the doors.

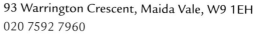

The main room is on the right and has a grey marble-topped counter with unusual, bulgy pilasters and lozenge decoration. Grey marble also appears in the columns of a three-bay arcade which marches across the right-hand side of the room, embracing the generously scaled staircase to what is now the upstairs restaurant. Some of the windows have lively stained glass, while over the servery is a semi-circular canopy, decorated with Art Nouveau-style paintings of naked ladies. More such paintings, with the signature Colin Beswick 1965, appear on the back wall and are meant to evoke the unlikely story that has grown up that this was once a brothel.

The left-hand room was once clearly divided into three as the patterning in the ceiling shows. The lowest status part has matchboard wall panelling and an ornate, much decayed mirror advertising Bass pale ale. Other things to note are the attractive and unusual high-level chequerwork glazed screens, the skylight over the first-floor landing and the deep, decorative cornices on the first floor.

Nearby: another good pub to take in is the Prince Alfred, just down the road, for its amazing display of Victorian screenwork. There's nothing quite like it in the country.

WARWICK CASTLE ㉔

6 Warwick Place, Maida Vale, W9 2PX
020 7432 1331
Grade II listed.
Tube: Warwick Avenue.
Real ale.

Despite some modernisation, this pleasant and relaxed pub, tucked away in a quiet side street, still has a good many Victorian features. Outside, don't miss the stunningly prominent iron lamp bracket – it's a good example of a feature often employed at Victorian pubs to advertise their presence. Street lighting was usually poor or non-existent and pub lamps acted like a beacon for prospective customers. The windows to the main bar have both strikingly large etched panes and some small stained glass panelled details. The entrances are embellished with tiled flooring.

Inside, the bar counter is quite an unusual affair with recessed panels, bold ornate brackets and a prominently project-

Above: **Stucco façade of the Warwick Castle**

Below: **Warwick Castle, tiled entrance lobby**

ing top tier. The bar-back, however, is modern but in keeping. The walls are largely covered in matchboard panelling above which is a delicate frieze. A second room on the left has a grey- and opal-coloured marble fireplace with unusual detailing. The appearance of the main bar is sadly marred by the unfortunate clumsy modern structure placed on top of the bar counter. The rear room of the pub has probably been brought into use in relatively modern times.

History nearby: Little Venice on the Regent's Canal has for a long time been popular with artists including Lucian Freud.

Above: **Bar-back inside the Cock & Bottle**

COCK & BOTTLE
(formerly Swan) 25

17 Needham Road, Notting Hill, W11 2RP

020 7229 1550

Not listed.

Tube: Royal Oak; Bayswater.

Real ale.

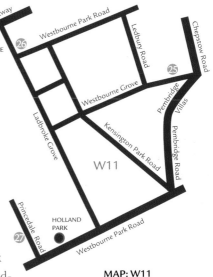

MAP: W11

This friendly, street-corner mid-Victorian pub has one outstanding feature – a bar-back of exceptional ornate- ness. It has a series of round columns with florid Corin- thian capitals below a broad frieze terminating in a band of ornament. The various round-headed projections on the columns have long been a mystery. Near the bottom of each is also a short round stub. And if you take a close look at the servery you'll see it has been cut back around the mod- ern opening to the inner room. A column has been removed. On the underside of the cornice you'll spot a hole. It's possible that all this means that there was once a gravity-feed system for spirits and wines (housed above the bar) which were fed down the pipes in the hollow columns to cocks on the stubs. Note also the pretty stained glass panels of swans which relate to the old name of the pub which changed in the late 1980s. The snob screens to the rear room are a modern bit of re-Victorianisation.

History in the area: Opposite is the huge pile of St Mary of the Angels, a Catholic church begun in 1857 which grew and grew, finally taking its present form in 1887. It was built at the instigation of Henry Manning who became the second bishop of Westminster in 1865 and later a cardinal. The church initially served a largely Irish population.

ELGIN ㉖

96 Ladbroke Grove, Notting Hill, W11 1PY
020 7229 5663
Grade II listed.
Tube: Ladbroke Grove.
NI Part Two.
Real ale.

A pub with some spectacular Victorian ornamentation, situated on the corner of a busy junction near to Ladbroke Grove tube station. Three distinct rooms are still clearly discernible although they are now interlinked. The star performer is the room in the northern part which is screened off from the corner bar by a wonderful timber and glass screen of exceptional exuberance. Then there is a bar-back of rare richness, embellished with 17th-century detailing, gilded mirrors and a frieze of bas-relief apples. On the side wall are more coloured tile strips and gilded mirrors displaying foliage, hops, butterflies and birds in flight.

The counters are original too and have doors to allow the servicing of the beer engines in times gone by. At the back of the pub is a large lounge with a rounded counter and fielded dado panelling round the walls. It has a skylight over the rear part. A sadness at this pub is the modern replacement in the corner bar of the Victorian bar-back by a modern one with metal uprights.

PRINCE OF WALES ㉗

14 Princedale Road, Holland Park, W11 4NJ
020 7313 9321
Not listed.
Tube: Holland Park.
Real ale.

This being fashionable Holland Park, this late-Victorian pub has moved upmarket – hence the trendy colours and (inevitable) ill-assorted mixture of non-pub seating. Yet it does retain a great deal of its original late-Victorian layout, glass and, remarkably, screenwork. It can be approached either from Princedale Road or from an entry on Pottery Lane. From either direction you are faced with a fine display of etched, patterned glass. From the Pottery Lane side there are two huge windows with the Prince of Wales's feathers and his motto 'Ich Dien' (I serve).

There are also doors with glass naming the rooms to which they led – public bar (right) and saloon bar (left). The Princedale Road side has two doors specifying 'saloon bar'.

Inside you will find an island servery whose counter front has small fielded panelling. No doubt there was an ornate stillion in the centre of the servery but, sadly, most of this has been stripped out. The interior space is divided up by a couple of screens with etched glass, a rare feature for a pub that kept up with late 20th-century change. The door glass names do not fully make sense today ('saloon bar' and 'public bar' glass lead to a single space) so we may imagine that more screenwork once divided the pub up into three small areas of the type so loved by Victorian drinkers.

History in the area: In the early 19th century the area near Pottery Lane, as its name implies, was the heart of brick and tile-making from the local clay. There is still a tile kiln on nearby Walmer Road. The area was also inhabited by pig farmers, hence the area's nickname became the Potteries & Piggeries.

Holland Park is not a park but an area of west London, most of which used to be the grounds of a 17th-century house called Holland House. In the 19th century many artists and art collectors lived here including Lord Leighton whose studio house, Leighton House (now a museum and art gallery), is at 12 Holland Park Road.

DUKE OF KENT (formerly Kent Hotel) 🏆

2 Scotch Common, West Ealing, W13 8DL
020 8991 7820
www.thedukeofkent@fullers.co.uk
Grade II listed.
Railway Station: Castle Bar Park.
Real ale.

Below: **1920s façade of the Duke of Kent**

An imposing suburban Fuller's house rebuilt in 1929 to designs by the excellent pub architect T H Nowell Parr and dominated externally by three gables on the rendered frontage. Although the pub has been modernised internally the original arrangements are still very much in evidence, especially along the front. Here there are three distinct rooms with internal partitions, the pair on the right even retaining a doorway between them. Needless to say each of the rooms had its own external entrance.

Above: **Etched glass on the exterior of the Prince of Wales**

Top Right: **Screen with etched glass inside the Prince of Wales**

Right: **Duke of Kent interior**

Above: **Tiled fireplace in the Forester**

Left: **Porticoed exterior of the Forester**

The wall panelling remains as does the bar counter although the fitting behind seems a modern replacement. In the windows there is some very typical, attractive dimpled glass that was popular with pub-builders around 1930. At the rear the counter is original. The back parts were extended in 1934 by Hall Jones & Partners to Parr's design. There is a large, hemispherical skylight but there has been extensive opening up and the spaces are now rather confused. However, they offer a pleasant prospect over the large garden.

History on the spot: The pub was built on the site of Castle Hill Lodge, a 27-acre site with a house (gone by 1840) owned by Edward, Duke of Kent, fourth son of George III and the father of Queen Victoria. The pub was known as the Kent Hotel until 2003.

MAP: W13

FORESTER

2 Leighton Road, West Ealing, W13 9EP
020 8567 1654
Grade II listed.
Railway stations: Northfields, West Ealing.
NI Part One.
Real ale.

A fine example of Edwardian suburban pub-building, erected in 1909 to designs by T H Nowell Parr for the Royal Brewery of Brentford. Parr provided a most distinctive piece of architecture, notable for its columned porticoes, green-glazed brickwork and prominent gables.

In all there are four rooms. There were originally five plus the (disused) off-sales on Seaford Road, but two rooms were combined to form the public bar. There are two rooms facing Leighton Road and one of these has the remarkable distinction of perhaps possessing the only historic bell-pushes for waiter service in a London pub – they have the word 'BELL' above them! Apart from their rarity, they are curious in that there is a perfectly decent bar counter in this room where able-bodied drinkers might quite reasonably have been expected to order their drinks!

There are some fine furnishings at the Forester. The servery still has its original counter and bar-backs which display a number of Tudor arches, a favourite motif of Parr's. There are a couple of Edwardian fireplaces complete with green tilework and in the public bar there are long-defunct remnants of gas lighting. There are also some delightful floral Art Nouveau-style stained glass panels in the windows, and there are doors in the counters for gaining access to service the beer engines in former times. The rear lounge is given over to well-regarded Thai food.

History across the road: The allotments on the eastern side of Northfield Avenue have been there since 1832. The allotments were established next to market gardens and orchards which proliferated in this area.

MAP: W14

COLTON ARMS ㉚

187 Greyhound Road, Earl's Court, W14 8NX
020 7385 6956
Not listed.
Tube: Barons Court.
Not listed.
Real ale.

There's nothing else quite like the Colton Arms in this guide. It's a local drinkers' pub in a modest, rendered Victorian building but its interior is a cross between a museum and a museum piece in its own right.

The drinking area wraps round the servery on three sides and is a time-warp of 1950s/1960s fitting-up. The style of much of what you see has sometimes been called 'publican's rustic', a deliberate attempt at rustic nostalgia with chunky woodwork, false ceiling beams and rough stonework.

Facing you on arrival is the bar counter and its slices of tree trunks on the upright face. There is lots of false half-timbering but the most surprising thing is the reused carved woodwork from old pieces of furniture. It seems that when such heavy, overblown carving was deeply out of fashion it could be bought up cheaply and so pieces found their way here.

History on the spot: It is thought that the Colton in the pub name was one George Colton who made a living as a clay pipe maker before turning to pub-keeping in the mid-19th century. Numerous fragments of pipes have been found here.

Below: **Colton Arms exterior**

Outer West

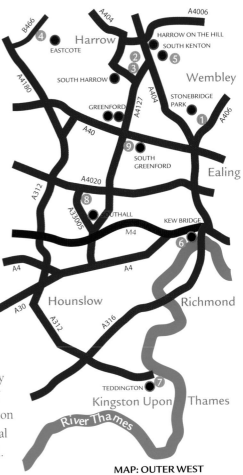

MAP: OUTER WEST

HEATHER PARK HOTEL ❶

Heather Park Drive, Alperton, HA0 1SN

020 8795 5654

Not listed.

Railway station: Stonebridge Park.

One of the many plain, neo-Georgian pubs built to serve the burgeoning estates around inter-war London, in this case one that has not improved with keeping. It lies at a point where several roads meet and its flanks are cranked backwards to follow the lines of the adjacent roads. The interior, like the external architecture, is simply and cheaply done but has not been completely opened out. The least altered part is in the centre with a long straight servery and two rooms of differing sizes. The left-hand one of the pair has veneer wall panelling which also appears on the bar counter and elsewhere. The bar-back is original but, like the rest of the work, is simple and functional.

On the far left-hand side is what is now a games room but this would, no doubt, originally have been a lounge. A similar room lies on the right-hand side but this has now been much altered and turned into a restaurant area specialising in excellent Indian food. In turn this area has been knocked into a further space beyond which is thought to have been an off-licence shop linked to the pub.

An unusual sight nearby are the motorcycle enthusiasts who congregate with their machines, especially at weekends, just north of the North Circular Road at the famous Ace Café.

History nearby: Just to the south is the Grand Union Canal which was formed in 1929 by the amalgamation of several canal companies. Originally this particular stretch was a branch of the Grand Union Canal to Paddington Basin: it opened in 1801 and joined the main route, connecting the Thames and the Midlands, near Hayes. To the north is the West Coast mainline railway which opened in 1838 as the London & Birmingham and was the first line into London.

Below: **Heather Park Hotel interior**

CASTLE ❷

30 West Street, Harrow, HA1 3EF
020 8422 3155
Grade II listed.
Tube and railway station: Harrow-on-the-Hill.
NI Part One.
Real ale.

Above: **Half Moon interior**

Below: **Half Moon saloon entrance**

Not far from Harrow School, the Castle was built in 1901 and has kept most of its original layout, the only real change being shown by an unused door down the side passage. Now the Castle consists of three rooms, the largest of these split by a screen with a low service door for staff to get from one part of the pub to another. On the right is a smaller room with a tiny hatch to the servery. Behind this is a further room with a large hatch to the servery. At the back is the final room with wood-block flooring and imitation panelling on the walls. The counter is the original one and so is the simple back fitting. The fireplaces look like modern insertions. Outside there is attractive ironwork over the main entrance and a mosaic floor panel with the pub's name.

History in the area: Harrow School was founded for local boys in 1572 by a yeoman called John Lyon but was not built until 1608-15 (the architect rejoiced in the name Mr Sly). In 1819-21 the architect C R Cockerell doubled the size of the original building and from then on additions have been built to the designs of several architects and designers including Giles Gilbert Scott, William Burges and Sir Herbert Baker.

HALF MOON ❸

1 Roxeth Hill, Harrow, HA2 0JY
020 8422 0209
Not listed.
Tube: South Harrow.
Real ale.

This is a highly striking piece of architecture – an asymmetrical, picturesque design involving lots of half-timbering, ornamental plasterwork, and other details consciously evoking the romantic days of 'olde Englande'. Plans were submitted in February 1892 on behalf of the Royal Brewery, Brentford, by a Mr S Wood-bridge of Brentford, and it was opened the following year.

Right: **Edwardian exterior of the Castle**

Below: **Original counter and screen inside the Castle**

The interior has three rooms whose irregular plan reflects the awkward site. The one in the angle of the roads is particularly oddly shaped: don't miss the extremely unusual and pretty tiled niche with a stained glass window showing a flowering pot-plant. To the left of this room is a delicious little snug with a concave-shaped counter front (complete with two doors which no doubt originally enabled servicing of the beer engines). The largest room – the saloon – is entered off Roxeth Hill and comes in three parts, a charming space in the front window and two further back. All the ceilings in the pub have deeply recessed panels. As for the other counters and bar-backs these are to a large extent modern work. The same is true of the gents' loos, which occupy the site of a former off-sales compartment. Don't miss the area outside: a large alcove recessed into former stables, designed for Edwardian clients to sit outside and take the air.

History nearby: In Bessborough Road lies Roxeth Farmhouse, a 17th-century weatherboarded building, a lone survivor from when this was once a farming area.

<< *LEFT HAND PAGE:*

'Olde worlde' interior of the Case is Altered

CASE IS ALTERED ❹

Eastcote High Road, Eastcote, HA5 2EW

020 8866 0476

Grade II listed.

Real ale.

Below: **Case is Altered 19th-century façade**

In its leafy surroundings, this is more like a country pub than a town one. Part of the right-hand side may date back to the 16th century but outside is mainly a remodelling after a fire in 1891.

Inside there is a deliberate attempt, probably dating from the inter-war years, to create an 'olde worlde' feel. This is especially apparent in the smaller and lower of the two rooms with its hefty black ceiling beams and imitation half-timbering. The doors and some of the panelling have a deliberately rough texture but this is actually synthetic material. The same manner of work continues, though with a little less bravura, in the larger, L-shaped bar. Both rooms have brick fire surrounds built of small red bricks. It is possible that there has been some degree of rearrangement in the post-war period and it seems unlikely that both rooms would originally have had the largeish panelled counters they do today.

LONDON'S PAST BREWERS

by Martyn Cornell

London was once one of Europe's great brewing cities, its big breweries feted and famous and, until well into Victoria's reign, the largest in the world.

The rise of massive breweries in London began around 1720 with the development of Porter, a strong, dark brew, which was the first beer that could be mass-produced on any large scale. Indeed, Porter almost demanded large-scale production, since its perfection came from being matured from a year or more in

One of the great porter vats at Barclay Perkins' brewery in Southwark. *Martyn Cornell collection*

large wooden vats of a size only the wealthiest brewers could afford to build and fill. London's semi-hard water is particularly suited to brewing dark beers and by the 1780s the capital's brewing scene was dominated by the twelve biggest Porter brewers, who made half of all the beer brewed in the capital, with the rest left to another 130 or so smaller producers.

The partners in the big porter breweries were extremely wealthy men. They included the Whitbreads of Chiswell Street, on the northern edge of the City, one of two centres of brewing in the capital; their great rivals at Barclay Perkins's Anchor brewery in Southwark, London's other big brewing centre; the owners of Truman's brewery in Brick Lane, in the East End; the Calvert family in Upper Thames Street, alongside where

Charing Cross station now stands; Henry Meux, whose brewery at the bottom of Tottenham Court Road is now covered by the Dominion Theatre; and the owners of the Red Lion brewery by St Katharine's Dock. All bought themselves country estates in the surrounding counties and many of them became MPs.

By 1815 the proportion of London's beer made by the great Porter brewers had grown to three-quarters. But as the 19th century progressed, Porter became less popular, and its replacement, mild ale, was made by a different set of firms. A handful of big ale brewers grew up: Charrington in Mile End; Mann nearby in Whitechapel; Courage at Bermondsey, diagonally opposite the Tower of London; and Goding's Cannon brewery on the north side of Knightsbridge, with Hyde Park behind it. However, local residents managed to get the Knightsbridge

Meux's brewery in around 1830. It lay at the corner of Oxford Street and Tottenham Court Road where the Dominion Theatre now stands. *Martyn Cornell collection*

Barclay Perkins' brewery on the south side of the River Thames in Southwark, for a long time the biggest brewery in London and the world. *Martyn Cornell collection*

brewery closed in 1841 – the Godings opened another establishment, the Red Lion brewery, on the banks of the Thames at Lambeth, where the Royal Festival Hall now is.

Meanwhile one of London's smaller brewers, Hodgson's of Bow, had been pioneering another type of beer. By the 1790s they had an export trade selling beer to the captains of the East Indiamen ships, who sailed from nearby Blackwall docks. These captains sold this beer to homesick employees of the East India Company in places such as Bombay and Madras. One beer in particular seemed to improve miraculously on the hard three- to four-month sea journey from Britain to India – a strong, pale, bitter ale which became known as India Pale Ale or IPA for short.

In the 1820s brewers from Burton-on-Trent began brewing IPAs in rivalry to Hodgson, and because Burton's own hard waters are better suited to making pale, hoppy ales, they began to capture the growing market from the 1840s for bitter beer. Several London brewers, such as Ind Coope in Romford, and Truman's, retaliated by opening their own branch breweries in Burton which is why many former Truman pub frontages still declare 'London and Burton Ales'.

A matchstriker advertising Whitbread's IPA from around 1910. *Martyn Cornell collection*

London's brewers had originally secured the trade of publicans via loans – clever pub landlords would have one loan from a Porter brewer, another from an ale brewer and a third from a distiller. Gradually, however, the loan system changed to outright ownership of pubs – tied estates. By the time the vast majority of London pubs were owned by brewers, the only way to expand was to buy out rival breweries and from the 1890s brewery numbers began to fall in consequence. The first big merger was between three of the former porter giants, Watney's of Pimlico, near Victoria Station, Combe's, in Covent Garden, and Reid's of the Clerkenwell Road, in 1898.

There were still around 140 breweries in the Greater London area in the 1890s. However, numbers crashed to just a couple of dozen by the start of the 1950s. Then rising property values and the problems of London's traffic squeezed the life out of even the biggest brewers. Today, of the old-established London breweries, only Fuller, Smith & Turner of Chiswick and the former Phillips & Wigan brewery at Mortlake, bought by Watney's in 1898 (and now brewing Budweiser) are still open.

Truman's London brewery traced its history back to 1666. The firm acquired Phillip's Brewery in Burton and brewed there until 1971. The London site ceased brewing in 1989

75

Above: **1930s interior of the**
Windermere

Above: **Express Tavern clock**

Below: **Express Tavern**
mid-Victorian interior

WINDERMERE ⑤

Windermere Avenue, South Kenton, HA9 8QT
020 8904 7484
Grade II listed.
Railway station: South Kenton.
NI Part One.
Real ale.

Right by South Kenton station this is a good place to see how a typical large, inter-war suburban pub was planned and fitted up. It was built in 1938 or 1939 and is a large, red-brick, Dutch-gabled structure.

There are three bars. The public bar, facing Windermere Avenue, is only used for parties and other functions. On the station side there is a saloon bar with a lounge behind. Original features include the large inner porches, bar counters, back fittings, wall panelling, wavy cornices, doors between the saloon and lounge, fireplaces (charming pictorial tiles with windmills in the saloon fire surround), tiles and fittings in the loos, and, in the saloon, an advertising mirror over the fireplace with Courage cockerel and a clock – the shape of the top reflects that of the gables outside. The only significant change is the loss of the off-sales compartment which has been incorporated into the public bar. The fixed seats are additions and the superstructures on the saloon and lounge counters look like work of the 1950s or 1960s.

EXPRESS TAVERN ⑥

56 Kew Bridge Road, Brentford, TW8 0EW
020 8560 8484
Not listed.
Railway station: Kew Bridge.
Real ale
Closed weekday and Saturday afternoons.

A popular pub for real ale drinkers, the Express was rebuilt in mid-Victorian times and old photographs show three original entrances. Now the sole, central doorway leads into a lobby with a mixture of Victorian and (perhaps) 1930s glazing. The right-hand room retains its original counter which, until rearrangements in 1994, stood further forward so creating a very narrow drinking area. The bar-back is ornate but, strangely, comes in two different parts, the left-hand portion being claimed as an import at some stage, though it is hard to understand what has been happening. The doorway to the former landlord's parlour has a fascinating double-sided clock over it, surrounded by brown painted and gilt glazing bearing the name of the pub. This decoration suggests a date of about 1870 and, if so, then perhaps we have here some of the earliest surviving pub fittings in London.

The left-hand room has a fine marble fire surround and original counter. The third room behind was remodelled in Tudor style in 1932 judging by the date scratched on a ceiling beam. A curious feature is the little peep-hole in the door to the serving area. Apparently this was used to call for drinks when the room was in use for private functions, for example, meetings of the brethren of the Royal Antediluvian Order of Buffaloes whose horns still hang proudly over the door to the front bar. The initials RA incised twice on the beams are of Robert (Bob) Aldington whose family acquired the pub back in 1882 and still own it to this day.

History nearby: The Kew Bridge Steam Museum is the former premises of the Metropolitan Water Works Company. Its most prominent feature is the Pump House Tower built in 1867 by Aird & Sons. It is over 60 metres high.

BUILDERS ARMS

38 Field Lane, Teddington TW11 9AS
020 8255 4220
Not listed.
Railway station: Teddington.
Real ale.

Above: **Builders Arms window**

Below: **Inside the Builders Arms**

A delightful street-corner pub just off Teddington High Street, it was rebuilt, almost certainly, in Edwardian times and shows a marked contrast with earlier, Victorian ornateness. Outside the ground floor is distinguished with brown glazed brick, a band of blue-grey mottled faïence and some attractive designs in the window frames.

The pub consists of two rooms. The public bar, entered off Field Lane, is by far the smaller of the two while the saloon stretches back along Bridgeman Road. There is a modern arched cut-through between the two rooms. Both of them have some delightfully detailed glazing with pretty green leaves and other motifs, though, sadly, the main windowpanes are now plain glass. Both rooms also have beamed ceilings which were popular at the time to create a kind of 'olde worlde' effect. The public bar has a rather unusual semi-circular-shaped counter and an individualistically detailed bar-back. The counter in the saloon is straight and, with the bar-back, looks as though it might be an inter-war replacement. A prominent Tudor-style arch spans the width of the saloon. A charming detail not to be missed is the Art Nouveau-style spear-like recesses carved in the panelling which are probably a unique feature in pub ornamentation. There are two original fireplaces.

History nearby: In the late 1850s the author of *Lorna Doone*, R D Blackmore, bought a plot of land between Station Road and Field Lane where he built a house called Gomer House near the end of the present Doone Close. In the same area he ran a market-gardening business. The house was demolished in the 20th century and Doone Close, Blackmore's Grove, Gomer Gardens and Gomer Place were built and named after him and his extensive activities.

Above: **Three Horseshoes beamed interior**

Below: **Exterior of the Three Horseshoes**

THREE HORSESHOES

2 High Street, Southall, UB1 3DA
020 8574 2001
Not listed.
Railway station: Southall.

On a busy corner in the centre of Southall, the Three Horseshoes is a work by the noted pub architect T H Nowell Parr. It was begun in 1914 but the coming of World War I and hard times afterwards meant that it was not completed until about 1922. The exterior is a good one with a brown-tiled ground floor and jettied first floor which includes lovely bay windows.

The outside doors name the rooms within on bold brass plates: reading from left to right we have saloon, public bar and private bar. Another door on the South Road side is thought to have led to a jug-and-bottle counter but it is hard to make much sense of the geography as a corridor has been amalgamated with the private bar and there is some very confusing woodwork which shows that the counter has been altered and cut back. However, the rest of the pub is remarkably intact and a good, quite early, example of 'brewers' Tudor' with all rooms having mock half-timbering, beamed ceilings and their original counter and back fittings. The saloon is notable for its attractive alcoves behind Tudor arches (Parr usually worked a few Tudor arches into his woodwork).

History in the area: Since 1950 Southall has been home to a large South Asian community, mainly Punjabi, hence the proliferation of Asian shops and restaurants along nearby Broadway. On Park Avenue and Havelock Road is the largest Sikh temple outside India, the Gurdwara Sri Guru Singh Sabha.

BRIDGE ⑨
Western Avenue, Greenford, UB6 8ST
020 8566 6246
Not listed.
Tube: Greenford.
Railway stations: Greenford, South Greenford.
Real ale.

Above: **Bridge Hotel exterior**
Below: **Bridge Hotel – some of the 1930s interior still survives**

Opened in 1937, this pub was built as a smart roadhouse to serve the comings and goings along the busy A40. It has changed drastically over the years and now functions primarily as a hotel although anyone is welcome to use the bar (after they have negotiated the gated access). The pub's central room is still well worth a look, despite changes elsewhere. Lying on the rounded corner of the pub, it is a quadrant-shaped room with counter, bar-back and canopy over and is mostly original. There are also appealing wedge-shaped alcoves towards the outside, two on either side of the Tudor-style fireplace (above it a much-darkened picture of Old Greenford Bridge before the A40 was invented). Until recently the alcoves had interesting wedge-shaped tables which have been ripped out in favour of plush seating. On the right the sliding door has also gone but the room beyond still has much of its 1930s panelling. Some panelling also remains in the left-hand room, now much opened towards the hotel.

History nearby: Despite the 20th-century roadscape which dominates the area, Oldfield Lane South boasts two old buildings: the grade I-listed Holy Cross church and the grade II Betham House, formerly a school, founded in the late 18th century by the Reverend Edward Betham.

Left: **Flask façade**
Below: **Victorian painting in the Flask**
Bottom: **Etched glass , paintings and original bar in the Flask**

NORTH WEST

NW1 to NW11

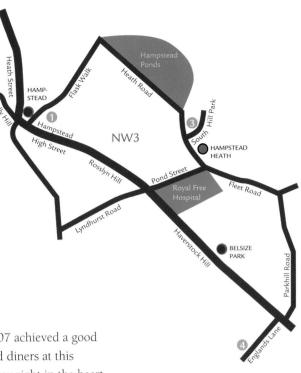

MAP: NW3

FLASK ❶

14 Flask Walk, Hampstead, NW3 1HG
020 7435 4580.
Grade II listed.
Tube: Hampstead.
Real ale.

A careful refurbishment by Young's in 2007 achieved a good balance between the needs of drinkers and diners at this famous Hampstead pub. It is up an alleyway right in the heart of Hampstead village and was rebuilt in 1873-4 by architects, Cumming & Nixon. The historic parts are at the front and what makes them special is the timber and glass screen dividing the two bars. On the saloon side it carries five chromolithographs of delightfully sentimental paintings by the Belgian artist, Jan Van Beers (1852-1927), whose name and partially obscured date '188?' appear on the one nearest the street. Van Beers specialised in this kind of work and it quite clearly appealed mightily to the landlord of the day. Above are etched glass panels with swirling patterns and birds.

The public bar (left) is now larger than it once was, having incorporated the former private bar (so-named in the side door glass). It's a pity that the front windows have been replaced with plain panes. The counter and bar-back are original and other features to note are the strips of tilework in both front bars, the extraordinary cast-iron column in the public bar, the metal fire surrounds (particularly ornate in the saloon), the decorated cornice and clocks on either side of the screen. The rear parts are almost exclusively modern.

History on the spot: The pub name reminds us that Hampstead was a spa in the 18th and 19th centuries (hence also the adjacent Well Walk). Water was bottled in Flask Walk and sold at the pub.

Above: **Holly Bush interior**

HOLLY BUSH ②

22 Holly Mount, Hampstead, NW3 6SG
020 7435 2892.
Grade II listed.
Tube: Hampstead.
Real ale.

The Holly Bush is a well known and popular Hampstead pub. There has been a good deal of alteration over the years with major extensions at the back and repositioning of old features such as etched glass but the character of the front parts is a delight.

The simply panelled bar counter and the coved bar-back are survivors from Victorian days. So too is a run of low screenwork and a baffle attached to the counter. This work clearly demarcated one part of the pub from another but the distinction has been blurred by the removal of the doors: the two outside front doors are also clear evidence of separate drinking areas inside. The right-hand part has full-height matchboard panelling and has been expanded into a tiny snug, the Tavern Bar.

On the left is a room described in the window glass as a coffee room which is entered by two doorways (one modern) leading off the main bar. This was no doubt for more refined customers who did not want to consume alcohol. This room has baffles to the seats and an ornate iron fire surround.

History nearby: The National Trust's Fenton House in Windmill Hill was built in the late 17th century by William Eades and has an important collection of early keyboard instruments. The house is named after one P I Fenton, a merchant from Riga, Latvia, who bought the house in 1793.

Below: **Curving exterior of the Magdala**

MAGDALA ③

2a South Hill Park, Hampstead, NW3 2SB
020 7435 2503
Not listed.
Railway station: Hampstead Heath.
Real ale.

This pub follows the gentle curve of the street. It went up in mid-Victorian times to serve the developing neighbourhood but is included in this guide for its 1930s makeover. You can see clear signs of this outside in the buff tile facing on the ground floor and the attractive strips of glazing in the windows. The left-hand room was extended but only the bar counter survives the rest having been given a dull modern look.

But on the right is a pleasant and remarkably intact room from the 1930s. The walls are elegantly panelled to half height and there is a low-key Art Deco frieze. The bar counter is panelled and follows the style of the wall panelling while the picture is completed by a Tudor-style pink marble fireplace.

History on the spot: The Magdala is famous as the place where Ruth Ellis shot her abusive lover, David Blakely, on Easter Sunday 1955 and went on, after a short trial, to become the last woman to suffer capital punishment in the UK. She went to the scaffold on 18 July the same year. Her story is told in a notice in the right-hand room.

Pubs in the area: If you have a moment, look in at the White Horse, 154 Fleet Road, just to the south. The prominent corner-site pub of around 1900 has impressive and highly unusual enamel-panelled ceilings. On the way, the Garden Gate has a good 'brewers' Tudor' exterior but has a modern exterior.

Above: **Panelled interior of the Magdala**

WASHINGTON
50 England's Lane, Belsize Park, NW3 4UE
020 7722 8842
Grade II listed.
Tube: Belsize Park, Chalk Farm.
Real ale.

The Washington effortlessly combines a relaxed modern atmosphere for eating and drinking with historic surroundings and has varied real ales. It is a prominent corner-site pub built in about 1865 for a developer, Daniel Tidey. The dominant feature outside is the bold first-floor windows with their alternating segmented and triangular heads.

The interior, although much pulled around in modern times, still retains a great deal of interesting Victorian work, probably from a refitting in around 1890. The building was a pub-cum-hotel and the lobby off Belsize Park Gardens has a floor mosaic proclaiming 'Washington Hotel' with the added temptation of 'Billiards' (ornamental door glass advertises 'hotel lounge' and 'hotel bar'). The first American president's bust appears in tiling above in a curious juxtaposition with some languid classical

Below: **Timber and glass fittings inside the Washington**

ladies. The name 'W Holman' here no doubt identifies the proprietor who redeveloped the place.

There are lots of remnants of screenwork including three bays of a full-height timber and glass partition. At the back are a series of the kind of back-painted mirrors depicting flora and fauna which seem to have been popular with late-Victorian pub owners. But the most extraordinary thing at the Washington is the high screen set above and forward from one side of the servery which is placed in the middle of the pub. It has glazing in its top parts and parts of the arcading survive.

History in the area: The area of Belsize Park is named after the former manor house and parkland developed in the 17th century for the Countess of Chesterfield. The present Belsize Park estate was put up between 1852 and 1878.

ASSEMBLY HOUSE ⑤

292-4 Kentish Town Road, Kentish
Town, NW5 2TG
020 7485 2031
Grade II listed.
Tube and railway station: Kentish Town.
Real ale.

<< *LEFT HAND PAGE:*

Top: **Assembly House, etched glass**

Bottom: **Ornate interior of the**

Assembly House

MAP: NW5

Below: **Assembly House exterior**

When it opened in 1898 this pub epitomised the grand, luxurious kind of establishment that was the hallmark of the great pub boom. The architects were Thorpe & Furniss. They provided an ambitious design outside in the Flemish Renaissance style which boasts a tourelle on the corner. There is ornate ironwork, polished stone facing on the ground floor and a series of prominent dormer windows.

The interior has undergone a pretty comprehensive modernisation yet there is still a lot of historic work to enjoy. You can still appreciate that the multiple entrances would have given access to a compartmentalised interior of the kind the Victorians liked. Even today, the front part (completely gutted) feels physically separated from the back. The best feature is the survival in the rear parts of one of the most elaborate panel-and-mirror displays anywhere. Set in tall rectangular panels are etched and cut mirrors with birds, foliage, swags and other decorative devices (note that a couple of large panels are later replacements – they lack the brilliant cutting of the Victorian originals). The

Left: **Bull & Gate interior** *Below:* **Sign showing a bull and gate**

Bottom: **Showy Bull & Gate exterior**

surviving bar-back, a tall, delicate piece, has similar work and is further embellished with touches of gilding. Other things to note are the lavish ceiling, cast-iron columns and the back room which has a large skylight to what was originally a billiard room.

BULL & GATE ⑥

389 Kentish Town Road, Kentish Town, NW5 2TJ
020 7485 5358
Grade II listed.
Tube and railway station: Kentish Town.
Real ale.

Now an Irish pub, the Bull & Gate was built in 1871 (see the helpful date-stone outside). It is a showy bit of architecture. Note external details such as the projecting single-storey part at the front, the shelly heads to the first-floor windows, the ornate fascia with the pub name and, of course, the plaster depiction over the entrance of a bull and gate.

There's much to enjoy inside too. Pride of place goes to the servery with its panelled counter and stunning array of decorated cut-glass mirrors with swirling sprays of foliage. The 'Linskey's' mirrors are modern but in the traditional style. The Bass mirror towards the back, however, is antique and has painted foliage and stuck-on lettering plus a Bass red triangle (draught Bass has long been popular here). A most unusual feature is the round arch between the two parts of the front bar – it has fluted jambs and, in the head, Neo-Classical urns and lion heads. The Lincrusta ceiling is an ornate piece of work too. Note also the fluted cast-iron columns which support the upper floors.

At the rear is a further room with an octagonal skylight: the glazing, sadly, has been replaced but the foliage swags around the drum are original. Like most of the ornament at this pub it has been picked out in various colours. This is perhaps rather garish but it means you can't miss all the Victorian detail. At the rear is a former billiard room, now used as a music venue.

History nearby: The London Forum, at 9-17 Highgate Road, was designed by J Stanley Beard and W R Bennett in 1934 as the Kentish Town Forum Cinema. After closing, in 1970, it became a bingo hall then a ballroom, later the Town and Country Club. In 1993 it was renamed the London Forum and has hosted many famous bands including Oasis and Hawkwind.

WHAT WE USED TO DRINK IN LONDON PUBS

by Martyn Cornell

In the days before so many London pub interiors were opened out to make one big space, which door you went through from the street – and thus what bar you frequented – determined much about you, including what beer you drank and how much you paid for it.

The public bar was for drinkers of Mild. Indeed, it was often nicknamed the 'four-ale bar', after the price of a quart pot of Mild, four (old) pence, which had led drinkers to order a 'pint of four-ale'. Mild, or mild ale, was a fresh, sweetish beer, generally (in London) dark, and lightly hopped, because it was not meant to stay in the pub cellar for long. It was not, before World War I, a weak beer, however: Courage, one of London's biggest mild ale brewers, brewed its XX Mild in 1891 to a gravity of 1060, which would have given a level of alcohol by volume (abv) of around 5.7% or so.

Mild was the most popular drink in London pubs from around the 1850s to the 1950s, the only beer you would be served if you went into the public bar and asked for 'a pint'. It was frequently drunk out of the curious salmon-pink pottery pint mugs eulogised

Early 19th-century porters enjoying their eponymous drink outside the White Hart, Knightsbridge. 'Entire' was a name often used for Porter. The pub was the tap for Goding's brewery nearby but was demolished in the early1840s to make way for the Albert Gate that now leads into Hyde Park. *Martyn Cornell collection*

by George Orwell in his 1946 essay about the perfect pub, the Moon under Water.

Mild had replaced Porter, the black, well hopped, often tart beer that had been the previous favourite of London's working classes since the 1720s. Porter was one of two great beer styles invented in London (along with IPA, or India Pale Ale). It grew out of the brown ales that London brewers had specialised in up to the end of the reign of Queen Anne (1702-14). The new brew rapidly became hugely popular with the thousands of street and river porters in London who loaded and unloaded ships in the Thames, and carried goods, parcels and letters around the city's streets, and it took their name as a result. It was, again, in its early years, a strong beer – 7% or so and aged for upwards of a year in huge vats, 22 feet or more high and with a capacity of 500 barrels or more.

Window glass at the Man of Kent, Peckham (p150) – but it's many a year since they sold mild here

The output of Porter hit its peak in London in 1823 when the capital's eleven or twelve big Porter brewers produced 1.8 million barrels. But from that point sales began to fall, dropping nearly a quarter in seven years. As Porter lost ground it became weaker. By the 1930s it was half its 18th-century strength and drunk mostly by old men. Production gradually ceased and the last London Porter brewer, Whitbread, stopped its production in 1941. Meanwhile the pre-eminence of Mild ale was being challenged by Bitter, the amber-coloured, hoppy brew that had started to arrive around the start of Queen Victoria's reign (1837-1901). If Mild was the drink of the working classes in the public bar, Bitter

PUBLIC BAR PRICES

DRAUGHT BEERS	HALF-PINT
Burton	7ᵈ
Bitter	6ᵈ
Best Mild Ale	5ᵈ
Mild Ale	4½ᵈ
BOTTLED BEERS	*Small Bottle*
Light Ale	7ᵈ
Brown Ale	7ᵈ
Oatmeal Stout	8½ᵈ

Guinness increased by 1½ᵈ and **Bass and Worthington** increased by 2ᵈ per Small Bottle.

Owing to War conditions, supplies of the above Beers may not always be available.

**Young & Co.'s Brewery, Ltd.,
Ram Brewery, Wandsworth**

A Young's of Wandsworth public bar price list from 1942 showing Burton (now known as Winter Warmer) and two types of mild. *Martyn Cornell collection*

was always the drink of the middle classes: even in 1850 *The Times* spoke of 'Bitter beer' being for 'the middle ranks'. It was more expensive than Mild and the staple of the saloon bar, where prices were always higher. But by the 1950s society generally was becoming more fluid. In 1958 *The Times* could now write: 'In many parts of the country, the drinking of bitter beers is on the increase. Traditionally Bitter is looked on as the bosses' drink. Any man reckons today he's as good as his boss. So he chooses Bitter.'

The decline in Mild from the start of the 1960s also meant a decline in the 'mixed' drinks that London beer drinkers have always been partial to: brown-and-Mild, a bottle of brown ale and a half pint of draught Mild (often drunk to cover the poor taste of the draught beer without the expense of all-bottled beer); Mild-and-Bitter; and Old-and-Bitter, or (rudely known as) 'mother-in-law', a mixture of Bitter and Burton ale. Burton, also known as Old or winter warmer, was a strong, sweetish beer darker than Bitter which was originally from Burton-on-Trent but very popular in London: at least eight London brewers were still making a Burton in the mid-1950s. Sales dropped even more rapidly than they did for Mild, however, as tastes changed to paler beers and by the 1970s there was only one Burton-style beer still being brewed in the capital.

Façade of the Two Brewers, Scotland Green, Tottenham with advertisements for Bass's Pale and Burton ales, and Reid's Stout c.1910. *Martyn Cornell collection*

LORD SOUTHAMPTON 7

2 Southampton Road, Kentish Town, NW5 4HX
020 7485 3106
Not listed.
Tube: Belsize Park.
Real ale.

A prominent corner-site community local, this was given a major refit between the wars, as indicated outside by the buff and mottled dark blue faïence facing. Although the dividing walls were progressively cut through between about 1973 and 1986, you can still gain a good sense of how the pub was laid out half a century or more ago. There were three rooms, each with its own external doorway and also an off-sales area entered from Grafton Terrace which remained in use until the late 1970s. There are plenty of inter-war features, including extensive wall panelling, exposed timbers in the ceilings (to create an 'olde worlde' effect) and the bar counter and back fitting.

The most intact part of the Lord Southampton is the left-hand rear area, which forms an intimate panelled space with its own glazed hatch to the servery. It's here that the door to the gents' leads off and into something unusual – a steel bridge spanning a small, enclosed yard below.

History across the road: St Dominic's Priory to the north has one of the largest Roman Catholic churches in London, 299ft long and built in 1874-83 by architect C A Buckler. South of the church the convent buildings, from the 1860s, are now houses.

Above: **Lord Southampton exterior**
Below: **Lord Southampton panelled interior**

Below: **Spectacular Victorian bar-back in the Pineapple**

PINEAPPLE 8

51 Leverton Street, Kentish Town, NW5 2NX
020 7284 4631.
Grade II listed.
Tube: Kentish Town, Tufnell Park.
Railway station: Kentish Town.
Real ale.

A tucked-away small corner local of around 1868 which was, fortunately, saved in the face of a closure threat in 2001 by a vigorous and effective local effort. The Pineapple has been opened up and there is now a single bar that wraps round the serving area. Here, you'll find a truly spectacular feature – the bar-back, a three-bay piece, and one of the best such examples from the mid-Victorian period anywhere. It's made of mahogany and has, at the top, panels advertising 'whiskies', 'brandies' and 'wines' in painted and gilt glass. Dividing the panels are florid Corinthian capitals. In between are etched mirrors with urns bursting with foliage and, below them – pineapples!

The bar counter seems original as is the marble fire surround on the left-hand side. There are also some fine mirrors with advertisements, a pretty cornice all around the front bar and dado panelling round the walls.

BLACK LION ⑨

274 Kilburn High Road, Kilburn, NW6 2BY
020 7624 1424.
Grade II* listed.
Railway station: Kilburn.
NI Part Two.
Real ale.

MAP: NW6

An imposing corner-site pub built in 1898 to designs by architect R A Lewcock it was rescued in 2003 from a very down-at-heel existence. It has a spacious, light interior enriched with some spectacular and appealing decoration. Pride of place goes to the series of four copper relief panels by designer F A Callcott depicting 18th-century men and women at leisure in the supposed predecessor of the present pub.

There is a deep and superbly ornate Florentine frieze in both main rooms and also a richly decorated ceiling. When built the main space would have been much more subdivided than it is now but there is still one screen surviving: it was moved to its present position in 2003 before which it was at right angles to the main road. There is a long, panelled bar counter and original bar-back. There are also fine etched windows on the side elevation of the pub – sadly, most have been removed from the front of the pub. The large room on the right (now a restaurant) was originally a music room.

History in the area: Kilburn used to be a minor spa. The actual site of the spa, south of the Black Lion, was where 42 Kilburn High Road now stands – as a plaque records.

Below: **Imposing exterior of the Black Lion**

Left: **Copper relief panel in the Black Lion**

Below: **Prominently displayed Charrington's signs at the Carlton Tavern**

Bottom: **Carlton Tavern interior**

CARLTON TAVERN ⑩

33a Carlton Vale, Kilburn, NW6 5EU
020 7372 0822
Tube: Kilburn Park, Maida Vale.
Station: Kilburn High Road.
Real ale.

This attractive inter-war pub is still very much a community local in what is now a sea of drab post-war housing. The ceramic advertising fascias leave no doubt as to who built it – the major East End brewers, Charrington's. Look out for the unusual sign down the side – 'Carlton Luncheon and Tea Room'. The original layout is still very apparent with a large public bar on the right, a smaller, better-class saloon on the left with the single-storey 'luncheon and tea room' still intact behind.

Each room retains its original counter and back fittings although, sadly, those in the public bar seem to have been subjected to a varnish stripper with dire results. As usual with inter-war pub fittings the details are restrained. A really attractive feature of the pub is the ceiling in the left-hand bar with its plaster foliage friezes and other decoration, now picked out in red and gold. There is similar decoration on a more modest scale in the luncheon room. Sadly most of the original window glass has been replaced.

History nearby: St Augustine's church (1870-7) is the architectural masterpiece in this area. This is one of the very greatest churches built during the Victorian Gothic revival and its architect, J L Pearson, designed Truro Cathedral (1880), Cornwall.

RISING SUN ⑪

137 Marsh Lane, Mill Hill, NW7 4EY
020 8959 1357
Grade II listed.
Real ale.

On high ground just on the edge of London, this feels more like a country pub than an urban one. It has been a pub since the 17th century but there is nothing one can see from that time. The core is just inside the front entrance – a delightful 19th-century servery with high-level screenwork. Along the right-hand side is a fixed bench and wall panelling with a shelf above. The

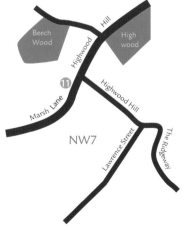

MAP: NW7

'stone' flooring was installed in a generally careful refit after a bus embedded itself in the front wall a few years ago. On the right, up a couple of steps is a cosy snug with more panelling and a fixed seat. The large, left-hand room is entered via a cut-through from the service lobby and dates from the 1950s. The 'barn' on the right is a function room and is pre-World War II.

History nearby: The early 19th-century Highwood House in Highwood Hill was once the home of Sir Stamford Raffles, founder of Singapore, governor of Java and a founder and first president of the Zoological Society of London. He died in 1826.

Above: **Rising Sun interior**

RICHMOND ARMS ⑫

1 Orchardson Street, St John's Wood, NW8 8NG
020 7723 5455.
Not listed.
Tube: Warwick Avenue, Edgware Road.

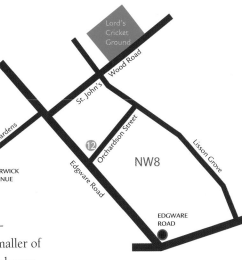

MAP: NW8

This part of the St John's Wood area was rede-veloped in the 1920s and, along with the new blocks of flats, came a community facility, the rebuilt Richmond Arms. It remains a remark-ably intact period piece.

The main façade to Lyons Place, where the pub is situated, has a central doorway to the private ac-commodation upstairs and two bars either side. The smaller of these, on the right, has its original fireplace and pretty decora-tive frames on the walls: its detailing is mirrored in the bar counter and bar-back. Very similar treatment reappears in the front left-hand room which retains its fireplace and the vestiges of a screen to a third, rear room. All three rooms have their original counters and back fittings; the rear room still retains its dumb waiter. The three original rooms are now all intercon-nected but the original arrangements and the old layout is easily understood. On the counter there are now gantry structures, which are in themselves period pieces. The lettering on the fronts is quintessentially 1960s or 1970s work and therefore from the time when such gantries started to become common-place features on pub bar counters everywhere.

History in the area: Tucked away in nearby Aberdeen Place is a closed pub, which is on CAMRA's National Inventory – the magnificent Crocker's Folly of 1898-9, soon to be a restaurant.

<< LEFT HAND PAGE
Above: **Rising Sun with adjoining 'barn'**
Below: **Richmond Arms with 1970s signage**

PUB NAMES AND SIGNS

The ornate sign outside the Lamb in Bloomsbury

Pubs go by a vast number of names, some ancient, some modern, some curious, some with a story to tell. The authors of a book on the subject in 1986* claimed a list of some 17,000 names and, despite a fall in pub numbers over the last couple of decades, the total still no doubt easily exceeds 15,000.

There is nothing particularly distinctive about London pub names and they reflect the huge variety encountered across the country. The two most popular names go back to medieval times. The Red Lion, with well over

500 cases across the country, is said to derive from the badge of John of Gaunt, Duke of Lancaster and England's most powerful man in the late 14th century. The Crown, with similar numbers, has long been a patriotic display of loyalty to the monarchy. Other ancient names are the White Lion (from the badge of Edward IV), the White Hart (from that of Richard II), the Rising Sun (a common heraldic emblem), Spread Eagle (heraldic) and various religious themes. These include the Angel, the Cross Keys (of St Peter), Olde

Mitre (p22), and Lamb (and Flag) – although the well-known Lamb in Bloomsbury (p11) is named after a Mr Lamb who established a water supply in the area in the 16th century (hence the name Lamb's Conduit Street).

Apart from the heraldic symbols already mentioned, there are other armorial bearings, including, in this book, the Colegrave Arms (p125), Argyll Arms (p35) and Joiners' Arms (p45). The latter refers to a livery company while the Hand & Shears (p19) refers to one of the ancient trades of the City. When it comes to the Builders' Arms (p77), we have to remember that this is a jokey play on the second word of the name.

Many pubs in this book commemorate the great and the good, no doubt revered by those conferring the name. Some are still well-known such as Queen Victoria (p43), Lord Beaconsfield (Disraeli) (p103) or Lord Nelson (p141); others now less so, such as the Victorian commander Lord Clyde (p140), Prince Frederick, a unique dedication to a son of George II (p161), or two of Queen Victoria's abundant offspring, Prince Alfred (p55) and the Princess Louise (p13).

Sport and pubs have long been closely linked and from days when blood sports were more acceptable we get the Dog & Duck (p37), Hare & Hounds (p181), and the Stag's Head (also heraldic) (p40). Local landmarks or circumstances provide the Viaduct Tavern, from Holborn Viaduct (p22), the Great Northern Railway (p109), the Flask (p81), the Highwayman (p184) or the Paxton's Head (p166).

Some names are completely modern. Name changes can provoke much indignation among locals but the process has been going on for centuries. Some modern examples are the Cittie of York (p9), a rebranding of a wine house which took its name from a long van-

The Flask in Hampstead

ished pub on the other side of the road; the Corrib Bar (p45) given an Irish name by the new owners of the Duke of Clarence; while Crocker's Folly (p174) is a renaming of the less excitingly named Crown and perpetuates one of the daftest pub myths that has ever been thought up.

Apart from the names themselves, signs are one of the distinctive features of the pub. Many names, especially in an urban area like London, are simply painted or affixed to the frontage, but a great many pubs still have pictorial signs attached at right angles to the building thereby providing a visual presentation of the name. This is in fact one of the most enduring characteristics of our pub heritage and goes back many centuries to a time when pictorial signs were put outside a great many more types of commercial establishment for the benefit of a largely illiterate populace. Outside central London, pubs that are set back from the road often have freestanding posts, which are then topped by traditional swinging boards.

Leslie Dunkling & Gordon Wright, A Dictionary of Pub Names *(Routledge & Kegan Paul).*

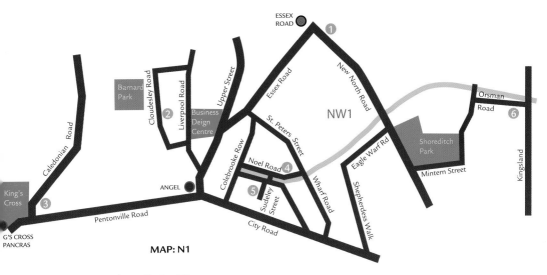

ESSEX ROAD ①   New North Road   Orsman Road ⑥

Barnard Park   Cloudesley Road   Liverpool Road   Upper Street   Essex Road   NW1   Kingsland

② Business Deign Centre   St. Peters Street   Eagle Warf Rd   Shoreditch Park

Caledonian Road   Colebrooke Row   Noel Road ④   Wharf Road   Mintern Street

King's Cross ③   ANGEL ●   ⑤ Sudeley Street   Shepherdess Walk

G'S CROSS PANCRAS   Pentonville Road   City Road

MAP: N1

NORTH

N1 to N22

CORLEY'S TAVERN ①

286 New North Road, De Beauvoir Town, N1 8SU

020 7288 1242

Railway station: Essex Road.

A small, cosy community pub, Corley's Tavern dates from 1953 and is one of London's early pub rebuilds following bomb damage during World War II. Post-war austerity meant that it is quite a plain building though there are some modest attempts at architectural detailing with raised concrete surrounds to the (original) windows and doors, and rock-faced stonework below the windows on the ground floor.

What is remarkable about it is that the two-room interior survives and is much as it was fifty years ago. The public bar faces the main road while the larger saloon is entered from Ecclesbourne Road. The other door on New North Road is marked private and leads to the landlord's living accommodation. Both public rooms have ply panelling on the walls and the two bar counters have the same fluted detailing in their fronts. When the pub was built in 1953, its freshness and the welcome relief it offered from post-war gloom, must have made it a popular new arrival.

<< LEFT HAND PAGE

Above: **Corley's Tavern interior**

Below: **Fine counter, with snob screens, in the Crown (p100)**

Below: **Corley's Tavern exterior**

CROWN ❷

116 Cloudesley Road, Islington, N1 0EB
020 7837 710
Grade II listed.
Tube: Angel.
Real ale.

A stylish Fuller's pub, with some sumptuous and unusual details, located in a smart part of Islington. It looks as though it was rebuilt in about 1900 and has attractive red-brick and polished, red granite and grey larvikite detailing. The outside walls are notable – simple thin screens of timber and huge expanses of glass. The lower panels of the windows have fine etched swirling and polished glass and the small panes at the top are also decorated. The servery sits right in the middle of the pub and was originally surrounded by a series of separate drinking compartments. Fortunately, enough survives to get a good sense of how things used to be. Each of the outside doors would have led to its own compartment and a couple of partitions survive. The counter is a fine piece with small panel details and a tapering base. It supports a long row of ten snob screens. There is another unusual two-bay curved screen on one end of the counter which originally held snob screens too. Finally, on the inner walls, don't miss the pretty frieze with cream and green strapwork decoration.

In the area: You may care to visit the popular Hemingford Arms, 158 Hemingford Road, Barnsbury, to admire the servery arrangements. There is a splendid stillion in the centre.

FLYING SCOTSMAN ❸

2-4 Caledonian Road, Pentonville, N1 9DU
020 7408 0226
Grade II listed.
Tube: King's Cross St Pancras.
Railway stations: King's Cross, St Pancras International.

Below: **Flying Scotsman façade**

Despite the sordid, blacked-out pub façade – thanks to this being a strippers' pub – there are things here of genuine heritage interest. But before venturing in, the external architecture, designed in 1900-1 by architects Wylson and Long, is worth a look. In front of the left and right entrances are the remnants of a mosaic telling us the pub was originally known as the 'Scottish Stores'. The interior is as grim as the exterior yet the central servery is surrounded by three distinct areas. Two screens survive as well as some etched and cut glass. The woodwork in the servery has a curious mixture of Gothic and Jacobean detailing and there is panelling around the pub walls with lithographs of hunting scenes.

History in a name: The Flying Scotsman was the name given by the London and North Eastern Railway (LNER) in 1924 to the Special Scotch Express between London and Edinburgh. The LNER Class A3 4472 Pacific locomotive built in 1923 to a design by Sir Nigel Gresley that ran on the route was also named the *Flying Scotsman*. The National Railway Museum now owns it.

ISLAND QUEEN ❹

87 Noel Road, Islington, N1 8HD
020 7704 7631
Grade II listed.
Tube: Angel.
Real ale.

The Island Queen, built in 1851, rises proudly above the adjacent terraces in this smart part of Islington. It was altered internally in 1889 and 1897 and, although various partitions around the central servery have been cleared away, much remains from this great age of London pub building.

The ground-floor frontage is a timber and glass screen and behind it is an extraordinarily high bar area. Historic survivals include the bar counter, the stillion in the middle of the serving area, vestiges of an inner porch on the left, two cast-iron columns and a full-height timber and glass screen forming a (now doorless) room to the rear right. There is a further screen on the right creating a corridor to the upstairs rooms. There is also some impressive etched and cut glass signed 'R Morris & Son, 239 Kennington Road. SE' who provided their wares to many a London pub in the late-Victorian years. Other features are the Lincrusta ceiling and pretty mosaic in front of the left and right-hand entrances. Tragically, most of the original window glass has been lost to clear replacements.

Note the impressive London Board School opposite, complete with its roof-top playground.

Above: **Exterior of the Island Queen**

Below: **Island Queen counter**

Above: **Inter-war woodwork inside the Prince of Wales**

Below: **Prince of Wales exterior**

PRINCE OF WALES

1a Sudeley Street, Islington, N1 8HP
020 7837 6173
Not listed.
Tube: Angel.
Real ale.

This down-to-earth corner-site pub is a real surprise in the early 19th-century streets of Islington. It was completely rebuilt in the 1930s and retains a considerable amount of original work. The exterior is quite plain but has some pretty herringbone brickwork and a series of doors that must have originally led to several internal spaces, probably including an off-sales area.

What really counts is the internal woodwork which shows how many hundreds of inter-war establishments must have looked before modern refurbishments. The walls are lined to two-thirds height with veneer which is then embellished with applied strips and painted bands to create panelled decoration. It spreads onto the walls of the two surviving rooms and behind the serving area. Much of the bar-back is original too. Other minor fittings to look out for are the delicate friezes throughout both rooms and the complicated metal openers to the upper lights of the windows. A dumb waiter descends into the barback.

History across the road: The pub overlooks the deep cutting of the Regent's Canal, opened in 1820 and which linked the Paddington arm of the Grand Union Canal to the River Thames at Limehouse.

STAG'S HEAD ⑥

55 Orsman Road, Hoxton, N1 5RA
020 7739 6741
Not listed.
Railway station: Essex Road.
Real ale.

This drinkers' pub is one of many built between the wars by major East End brewers, Truman's, in this case, to serve a 1930s housing estate. The ground floor is faced with mottled blue and brown tiles that were then very popular for pub frontages. It is quite small and originally consisted of two narrow bars either side of a servery plus a 'home sales' compartment (now disused, of course). The public bar is on the right (on the street corner), the saloon on the left. In the 1950s or 1960s an extension was added on to the saloon though it seems they couldn't quite get the tile match right.

The interior is characteristic of Truman's house style. Note their characteristic lettering advertising their oatmeal stout, Eagle ale, etc. on the woodwork and typical brick fire surrounds with small relief panels – the leaping stags found here also prance about in other Truman's pubs – and mirrors in the overmantels. The chequered spittoon trough found here is another frequent arrangement. The social (and price) distinction between the two sides is mirrored in the bar counters – commonplace matchboarding for the public bar and a more elegant streamlined effort in the saloon. Happily the toilets in both halves of the pub have not experienced modern refits and the tilework still appears as it did to those answering the call of nature seventy years ago.

History in the area: Gainsborough Pictures, a film studio founded in 1923 was located in a former power station in nearby Poole Street until 1951 and was where Alfred Hitchcock began his career. In 2002 the building was demolished and replaced by flats in 2004.

Above: **Stag's Head interior**

BEACONSFIELD

357-9 Green Lanes, Harringay, N4 1DZ
020 8800 2153
Not listed.
Railway station: Harringay Green Lanes.
Real ale.

MAP: N4

A down-to-earth pub, which, although opened out, still retains a remarkable amount of Victorian work. Its changes over the years have been carefully documented and a history at the pub enables us to follow its evolution. The Beaconsfield was built in 1886-7 to the designs of the obscure architects Alexander and Gibbon who drew upon 17th-century details for inspiration.

After the arrival of the third licensee in 1897 the internal arrangements were changed with the installation of the present island servery which was surrounded by a series of compartments. The plan was drawn up by John E Pinder. One partition was removed in 1904 by F J Eedle & Meyers, minor alterations

BEAUTY IN VICTORIAN CRAFTSMANSHIP

Patterned glass, decorated mirrors, rich 'plasterwork', coloured tiles and mosaics, ornate metalwork and tons of mahogany from the far-flung Empire all embellished the late Victorian pub. Many of the techniques had been around for generations but it was a combination of technological innovation, industrial production methods and unprecedentedly cheap transport that made them freely available.

1890s tilework at the Princess Louise, Holborn (p13)

GLASS

We still possess large amounts of magnificently decorated glass in pub windows, doors, and wall panels. Various techniques were used. Etching was carried out by the use of dilute hydrofluoric acid to create embossed glass. From the 1880s the advent of 'French embossing' by the use of various acids and chemicals allowed different tones to be produced and some of the finest products are to be found at the Princess Louise, Holborn (p13), and the Viaduct Tavern, Smithfield (p22). Gilding and colouring was also practised. We still have a number of delightful back-painted mirrors as at the Half Moon, Herne Hill (p159), the Alma, Wandsworth (p189), and the Bunch of Grapes, Knightsbridge (p172). There was an explosion of decorated advertising mirrors, superb examples of which exist at the Dog & Duck, Soho (p37) and the Tipperary, Fleet Street (p33).

TILES

There were great advances in industrial tile production beginning in the 1840s by firms such as Minton in Stoke-on-Trent and Maw at Benthall in the Ironbridge Gorge. Tiles were particularly well suited for lining pub walls, being hard wearing and easily cleaned. By the end of the century large tile pictures were sometimes commissioned for pubs such as the Dolphin, Hackney (p123) or the Ten Bells, Spitalfields (p120). The most notable supplier of these was W B Simpson & Sons who bought in blanks from Maw's and painted them before firing. Mosaic floors became

Late-Victorian decorative glass at the Red Lion, St James's (p167)

Frieze at the Black Lion, Kilburn (p91)

equipment to cope with the foreign hard-woods that were brought in to fit out the pubs of the day. Much of it was supplied by specialist firms who could fit out banks, shops, pubs and a host of other premises. Such a firm was Edwards & Medway of the Kennington Steam Joinery Works, Lambeth, who manufactured the cabinet work for the Assembly House, Kentish Town (p85). W M Brutton, who designed the exotic King's Head, Tooting (p186), usually used the firm of J Brown & Co.

popular for entrance lobbies and, sometimes, as at the Tipperary, for bar flooring.

'PLASTER' CEILINGS.

Many a Victorian pub is embellished with ceilings and cornices in high relief. Although sculpture was modelled in plaster, so much of what appears to be plasterwork is in fact imitation involving paper or canvas pressed or stamped into the required design. The best-known name is Lincrusta-Walton. A good example is at the Assembly House, Kentish Town (p85) where the supplier was, as Mark Girouard tells us in his book, *Victorian Pubs*, the Plastic Decoration Co, 'manufacturers of architectural decoration in fibrous plaster, a large stock of dry fibrous plaster always in stock, papier mâché, carton pierre etc.'

WOODWORK

The lavish decoration beloved of the Victorians for their pubs must have kept countless craftsman employed and they were equipped with mechanical

IRONWORK.

Ornamental ironwork was a feature in the more elaborate late-Victorian pubs. It was used, for example, to provide the supports for the monster lanterns that were used to light the outside of pubs and advertise their presence, such as at the Warwick Castle, Maida Vale (p60). Other pubs had a row of standard lamps in front of their façades as can be seen at the Crown & Greyhound, Dulwich (p155). Florid decorative ironwork was used in the heads of many a doorway to announce the name of the pub or the room to which access was being provided.

The saloon beckons at the Salisbury, Harringay (p106)

Above: **Beaconsfield interior**

were made in 1934 and further partitions were removed in 1953. The single space we have today was the work of Courage (Eastern) Breweries' chief architect, Mr Longstaff, in 1981 when the last remaining divisions were removed.

The Victorian work remaining consists of the spacious servery (with its stillion in the middle), the richly decorated ceiling, six cast-iron columns, curved lobby entrance on the corner, a considerable amount of etched mirrorwork towards the rear and some stained glass.

History in a name: The pub is named for Conservative politician Benjamin Disraeli (1804-1881). He entered Parliament in 1837 and was chancellor of the Exchequer briefly in 1852 and again in 1858-9 and 1867. Prime minister in 1868 and 1874-80, he became a close friend of Queen Victoria whom he persuaded to assume the title of Empress of India. He was made Earl of Beaconsfield in 1876.

Above: **Salisbury interior**

Below: **The grand exterior of the Salisbury**

SALISBURY ⑧

1 Grand Parade, Green Lanes, Harringay, N4 1JX
020 8800 9617
Grade II* listed.
Railway station: Harringay Green Lanes.
NI Part One.
Real ale.

One of the grandest of all pubs built during the great pub boom in the closing years of the 19th century. After years as a run-down pub it was given a careful refurbishment after 2002-3 which has returned it to its former glory. The Salisbury went up in 1898-9, the promoter being John Cathles Hill, a self-made builder and developer who is said to have made the designs himself. He was also responsible for developing large swathes of housing nearby. The Salisbury is a companion piece to Hill's similarly splendid Queen's Hotel in Crouch End (p110) and the plans of the two pubs are very similar indeed. The rich ironwork and the mosaics and tiling in the generous porches on the exterior of the pub give a foretaste of what to expect inside.

The most lavish room was the 'saloon' on the right and, although it has lost its skylight, the alcoves, plaster, mirrors and woodwork still make it very special indeed. At the rear the former billiard room retains its lovely skylight and is now used as a restaurant and function room. The remainder of the pub is taken up with two bars surrounding an island servery of epic proportions. Originally there would have been more drinking areas within the large L-shaped bar on the corner. The counter is a fine one with small, deep panels. Behind is a largely original back fitting, which bears pretty, delicate Art Nouveau painted details. The major and sumptuous addition in 2003 was the black and white marble floor in the corner bar.

History in a name: The Beaconsfield down the road is named for one Conservative leader, the Salisbury for another. Robert Cecil (1830-1903), 3rd Marquess of Salisbury, entered Parliament in 1853. Prime minister in 1885-6 and 1895-1902, unlike the Liberals, his government was sympathetic to the drink interest which created a climate in which pub-building flourished.

FLASK ⑨

77 Highgate West Hill, Highgate, N6 6BU
020 8348 7346.
Grade II listed.
Tube: Highgate.
Real ale.

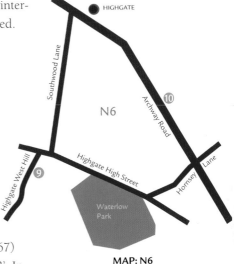

MAP: N6

Two buildings now forming one pub in an attractive leafy part of smart Highgate. The original, possibly early 18th-century, three-storey section (partly rebuilt about 1767) has a plaque noting an earlier incarnation, 'The Flask 1663'. In this part there are two old rooms with a servery between them. This has sets of impressive, well preserved glazed sash windows while the shelving and panelling inside seem of real age (possibly mid-19th-century if not earlier). The public can now walk between the two areas but originally they were separate as the surviving woodwork suggests. There was an extensive makeover in the 1930s from which time we have the plain counter front, spittoon trough, panelling and (now doorless) telephone booth. There are two typical 1930s fire surrounds with thin brickwork. The pub has expanded considerably to the left and rear and the atmosphere here is quite modern.

History on the spot: Pubs used to be focal points for many functions and community activities which have now migrated to specialised premises. The Flask was the place the local manorial court was held in the 18th century.

Below: **Inside the Flask, Highgate**

Above, top: **Great Northern Railway Tavern sign**

Above, bottom: **Great Northern Railway, etched glass**

Left: **Impressive glazing inside the Winchester**

WINCHESTER ⑩

206 Archway Road, Highgate, N6 5BA

020 8374 1690

Not listed.

Tube: Highgate.

Real ale.

Built in 1881 as part of a very distinctive parade of shops with housing above, it was then the Winchester Tavern and later became the Winchester Hall Hotel. Inside, the great feature is a massive, glazed-in office surrounded on three sides by the servery. Its windows have remarkably lovely, delicate etched glass with trails of foliage and depictions of flowers and birds.

Originally there would have been multiple rooms and drinking areas. Most of these have been swept away but one screen survives (just at high level) with yet more lovely glazing. At the rear, through an arch from the main bar, there is a room with a diagonally boarded ceiling. The counter is original and has a number of doors for servicing beer engines in former times. Don't miss the wonderful ironwork over the two entrance porches.

Nearby: If you are heading back into town on the bus, you may care to drop in at Phelan's Bar (formerly Mother Red Cap), 655 Holloway Road, near Archway station, for a striking display down the left-hand wall of large late-Victorian mirrors and some great surrounding tiling.

History in a name: The name comes from Winchester Hall, a late 17th-century mansion nearby. This and its estate were sold as the relentless tide of bricks and mortar engulfed the area following the arrival of the railway in 1867.

GREAT NORTHERN RAILWAY ⑪

67 High Street, Hornsey, N8 7QB

020 8340 4724

Grade II listed.

Railway station: Hornsey.

Real ale.

When originally built in 1897 this pub must have been a stunner. The architects were Shoebridge & Rising who were responsible for many a London pub. Here they produced a flamboyant essay in the Flemish Renaissance manner. The raised

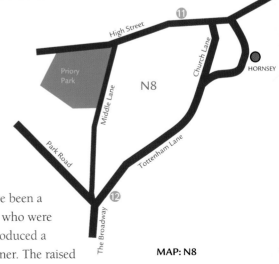

MAP: N8

RIGHT HAND PAGE >>
Opulent interior of the Queen's Hotel

Above: **Queen's Hotel stained glass**

Below: **Queen's Hotel entrance**

brick lettering, ornamental ironwork and the etched and cut glass give an expectation of splendours within.

The interior of the pub was remodelled in the late 20th century by the late Roderick Gradidge, one of the most sensitive architects of the time dealing with pub refurbishments. The front parts are now a single space but some sense of subdivision has been achieved by the reuse of the original fine glazed screenwork. The L-shaped servery still has its 1897 counter and the bar-back is lined with a series of lovely decorated mirrors. There is a skylight over the rear left-hand area.

Another, bigger skylight sits near the wonderfully gracious music room at the rear. It is spanned by two hefty tie-beams and has rich plaster friezes on the main walls and also below the skylight. The swirly decoration (similar to that in the main bar) on the coving looks as though it may be Gradidge's work as is perhaps the fireplace.

History in a name: The name comes, of course, from the east coast mainline railway, which thunders by a little to the east. The bill for the railway secured Royal Assent in 1846 and the main line to Doncaster was opened in 1852 as was the London terminus at King's Cross, then the largest station in England.

QUEEN'S HOTEL ⑫
26 Broadway Parade, Crouch End, N8 9DE
020 8340 2031
Grade II* listed.
Railway station: Hornsey
NI Part One.
Real ale.

An opulent hotel-cum-pub built in 1899-1902 at the height of the great pub boom and still a fine place to eat and drink. It's a companion piece to the magnificent Salisbury in Green Lanes (p106). Both were built by the developer John Cathles Hill, who is said to have acted as his own architect.

The layout is very similar to the Salisbury with a large servery in the centre surrounded by a series of rooms and compartments. There is a screen across the bar at the front. There is another screen just inside the entrance on the Elder Avenue side. On the right-hand side is a saloon with a couple of alcoves and a spectacular decorated plaster ceiling and half-height

panelling. The ceilings and deep friezes throughout the pub are immensely intricate in their decoration.

There are lots of other features to admire, notably the beautiful Art Nouveau-style glass with roses and other flowers. The bar counter is original and so is the circular entrance arrangement in the corner with a mosaic floor bearing the monogram of Mr Hill and Q for Queen's. Unfortunately the fitting in the centre of the servery has, for some reason, been replaced with modern work. The pub also suffers from an overpowering gantry atop the counter. A refurbishment in 2001-2 was a sensitive piece of work apart from the cutting of an opening in the screen.

Nearby: You may care to drop in at the nearby 1930s 'brewers' Tudor' Railway, 23 Crouch End Hill. It's been much altered but has a magnificent inglenook fireplace.

ARMY & NAVY

1-3 Matthias Road, Stoke Newington, N16 8NN
020 7275 8918
Railway station: Dalston & Kingsland.

This wedge-shaped, red-brick pub was one of many rebuilt by Truman's in the 1930s to upgrade the quality of their estate and, like the Rose & Crown, Stoke Newington (p113) is a good place to see something of their house style. Outside there are ironwork pub lanterns, a bow-fronted window, and attractive window glass with dimpled panes and pretty, coloured strips.

Like the Rose & Crown, the interior displays typical trademarks of Truman's inter-war fitting and furnishings. There is characteristic advertising lettering (see over the bar-back), brick fire surrounds with small relief panels (in this case a hunter and dog, knight on horseback, and a couple of galleons) and a very distinctive cream-coloured ceiling made up of Vitrolite panels (just as at the Rose & Crown). Originally the pub would have been divided up into a sequence of separate rooms by screens but these have now all gone. However, you can still see two different treatments in the bar counter detailing which signify separate drinking areas (the usual distinction being plain for the public bar, smarter for the rest). The bar-back is also original.

History in the area: St Matthias church in nearby Wordsworth Road was designed in 1851 by the great Victorian architect William Butterfield. Note its unusual saddleback crossing tower.

MAP: N16

Below: **Army & Navy interior**

ROSE & CROWN

199 Stoke Newington Church Street,
Stoke Newington, N16 9ES
020 7254 7497
Railway Station: Stoke Newington.
Real ale.

Above: **1930s Rose & Crown interior**

An ambitious Truman's pub of 1934 that sweeps elegantly round a corner. Exterior features to note are the lamps, a pair of fine metal inn signs, and glazed shop-window to display wares from the former off-licence. You can also trace the sequence of original rooms in the metal signs over the doors: right to left – public bar, private bar, outdoor sales, saloon and lounge.

Internally there is still a good feel of the 1930s layout since the screens dividing the various rooms survive in their upper parts. Do have a look at the light-shades. Extraordinary as it may seem, these appear original and different parts of the pub have different-shaped shades. The panelling in the interior is in classic Truman's style of the 1930s. Characteristics involve advertising lettering on the panelling naming some of the brewery's offerings, the chequered spittoon trough, light-cream-coloured Vitrolite panels in the ceiling, overmantels with Truman's mirrors inserts and doors in the bar counter to get at the beer engines. Note also some of the chairs, which are not unlike the 1930s survivors at the Fox and Pheasant, West Brompton (p176). The heavy-handed 'stone' flooring is clearly a product of the opening up of the pub.

BEEHIVE

Stoneleigh Road, Tottenham, N17 9BQ
020 8808 3567
Railway station: Bruce Grove.
NI Part One.
Real ale.

MAP: N17

A very good example of an unspoilt 'brewers' Tudor' pub, in this case a rebuild of 1927. The old layout is complete (apart from the removal of a screen) and you can fully appreciate how such a pub was meant to appear. The public bar (left) has an L-shaped panelled counter, wall panelling, two cased-in darts boards and three of the original benches. The glazed-in office

SNUGS, SNOB SCREENS AND VICTORIAN DRINKING HABITS

The pages of this guide are filled with references to pubs with multiple rooms and to others with screens that divide (or used to divide) the drinking space. People still expected a multi-room pub right up to the 1960s when the great trend to open up got going in earnest. Such pubs had a heirarchy of rooms from the public bar through to the saloon bar (or similar) and differential pricing of drinks to match. This hierarchy descended from the Victorians who were very sensitive to social stratification, people preferring to drink amongst others whom they regarded as their peers.

In some cases the original spaces may seem to have been ludicrously small but that's exactly how many late Victorians liked them when having a drink with their friends. The tiny snug at the Dove, Hammersmith (p49), is, reputedly, the smallest pub room in the country while the two unique wooden drinking boxes at the Barley Mow, Marylebone (p174: but currently closed), are full if four or five people squeeze in. It will seem incredible that the already tiny front bar at the Red Lion, St James's (p167) was once

A bank of snob screens at the Travellers Friend, Woodford Green (p133)

subdivided. Commonly, timber and glass screens divided up the open area around or in front of the servery and the two greatest survivors are to be found at the Prince Alfred, Maida Vale (p55) and the Argyll Arms, Soho (p35).

Snob screens are one of the most distinctive (and, to us, curious) survivals from Victorian pubs. They are small, square, swivelling glazed panels at eye level between the two sides of the bar counter. The best set survives at the Prince Alfred, Maida Vale (p55), but they are also found, for example, at the Lamb, Bloomsbury (p11) and the Travellers Friend, Woodford Green (p133). They were designed to provide a degree of privacy for the would-be better class on their side of the counter but could be turned should the staff need to know who the customers were and to allow face-to-face contact should any clarification, say, over a drink order, be needed.

Looking down into the tiny drinking boxes at the Barley Mow, Marylebone (p174)

survives but the off-sales is now disused. The spacious right-hand side still has its mock beams, panelling, large brick fire surrounds and light fittings. The sliding screen between the 'saloon lounge' (front) and 'luncheon room' (rear) has gone but the glazing above remains. There's a skylight over the rear area. One unusual feature is the numbering of every door (up to 20 in the luncheon room). It was standard practice to number rooms in pubs until the 1960s (as required for control purposes by Customs and Excise) but individual doors is another matter. A further curiosity is the fact that the 'wooden' panelling is nothing of the sort – feel it and tap it and you will find it is an imitation to create a Tudor effect on the sly.

Above: **Interior of the Beehive**

GATE (formerly Starting Gate) ⑯

Station Road, Wood Green, N22 7SS
020 8889 9436
Grade II listed.
Railway station: Alexandra Palace.
Real ale.

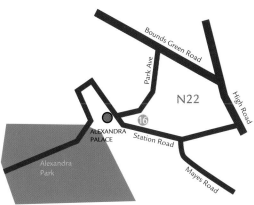

MAP: N22

Now a modern-atmosphere eating and drinking establishment, some considerable vestiges of this pub's rich, late-Victorian furnishings remain. Interestingly, this pub didn't start life as a pub but as the Palace Café, opened in 1875, the same year as Alexandra Palace. It turned into a pub by 1896 and was refitted by Richard Dickenson of St John Street, Adelphi, in 1899 – no doubt the date of much of what we see today.

Inside is a central servery from which compartments once radiated and the six outside doors show these were numerous and therefore small. The surviving screen panels are formed of timber and etched glass, the latter embellished with the small birds and swirling foliage that never failed to delight late-Victorian pub owners and customers. The panelled oak bar counter is Victorian as are the mirrors in the central stillion (although the structure itself is modern). The timber arch above, however, is Victorian, and spans two mighty, fluted cast-iron Corinthian columns. Another item of interest is the mosaic flooring marking out a former corridor leading from the St Michael's Terrace entrance. You will also find a well preserved bank of snob screens sitting on the counter.

Below: **Late-Victorian interior, the Gate**

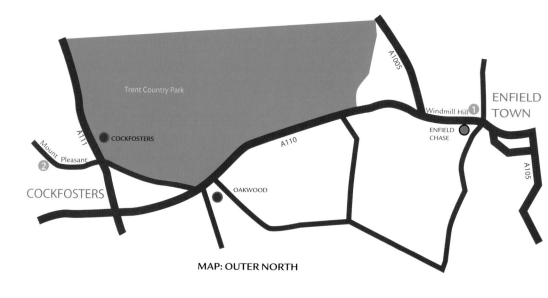

MAP: OUTER NORTH

Outer North

OLD WHEATSHEAF ❶
3 Windmill Hill, Enfield, Middlesex, EN2 6SE
020 8363 0516
Not listed.
Railway station: Enfield Chase.

Below: **Old Wheatsheaf exterior**

In 1905 this pub – then a beerhouse - changed hands and, judging by the embellishment, was probably remodelled soon after that. It has a particularly attractive ground-floor frontage with a couple of curved bay windows and brown glazed brick facing. The etched windows with their leaded heads (best appreciated from inside) come with delightful representations of a wheatsheaf and Art Nouveau-style flowers.

The 'jugs and bottles' department (named in the door glass) has gone but the pub still has two entirely separate rooms. The one on the right sports a very fancy fireplace and mirrored overmantel: the tiled strips with stylised tulips are, again, typically Art Noveau. The bar-back is plain and may be work of the 1930s while the plain matchboard counter (the same as in the other room) is hard to date. In the left-hand, single-storey room there is extensive three-quarter-height matchboard panelling. Here the fire surround is much plainer than next door. The pub was probably called the *Old* Wheatsheaf to distinguish it from another Wheatsheaf in Baker Street situated at the other end of Enfield Town.

History on the spot: Time was when landlords often combined pub-keeping with other occupations. Gary Boudier's book *A-Z of Enfield Pubs* tells us that in 1855 licensee William Collins is recorded as a beerseller and rat-destroyer. It seems logical to think that he also rounded up the little beggars for ratting matches which used to be a popular pub entertainment in which dogs (and occasionally humans) competed to kill the most number of rats in a defined period of time.

Above: **Art Nouveau interior of the Old Wheatsheaf**

JESTER ❷

150 Mount Pleasant, Barnet, EN4 9HE
020 8449 8379
Not listed.
Tube: Cockfosters.

This pub was built in 1958 to serve the surrounding housing estate and therefore dates from a time when pub-building eventually got going again after the hardships of the post-war years. It has rather more architectural ambition than most of the functional pubs of its day, having been built in the kind of vernacular revival that had been popular in the period between the wars – with broad, sweeping rooflines, dormer windows, tall chimneys and attractive brickwork.

Inside there are two rooms, a public bar to the front and a lounge down the right-hand side. The latter has been expanded by a cut-through into what was originally part of the private accommodation. The public bar retains some characteristic panelling with broad flat members and narrower hollows picked out in black. Such panelling recurs in the lounge but, sadly, it has been painted over as has the bar counter (the bar counter in the public bar is a grim bit of Formica refacing). But for a quintessential piece of 1950s design look at the tiled surround to the fireplace in the lounge – it contains a series of tiles showing the eponymous jester and images of wine glasses just in case you had forgotten you are in a pub!

Above: **1950s exterior of the Jester**
Below: **Jester fireplace**

Left: **Late-Victorian wall tiles in the Ten Bells (p120)**

Below: **Four-storey exterior of the Ten Bells (p120)**

EAST

E1 to E18

GOLDEN HEART ❶

110 Commercial Street E1 6LZ

020 7247 2158

Not listed.

Tube and railway station: Liverpool Street.

Real ale.

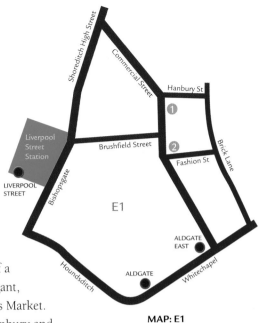

MAP: E1

A good, relaxed place to soak up the atmosphere of a typical inter-war pub. The Golden Heart has an elegant, three-sided neo-Georgian frontage facing Spitalfields Market. It was built by the major local brewers, Truman, Hanbury and Buxton, on a corner site around 1930 and is just a few yards away from the company's very different Ten Bells (p120).

This pub has two bars either side of a central servery but a blocked doorway in the centre indicates how the larger bar on the right is an amalgamation of two original rooms. This enlarged public bar is rather plainer than the other one but both have extensive panelling, brick fireplaces (note the Truman's eagle over a couple in the public bar) and Truman's house-style lettering for the advertising inscriptions running along the top of the panelling. Note also the pleasing dimpled and coloured glass in the windows. None of this is showy and represents one of the two main faces of interwar pub-building – the careful, restrained Georgian one as opposed to nostalgic 'brewers' Tudor'. The one real blemish here is the modern pot-shelf on the public bar counter.

History round about: Spitalfields Market was established in 1682 to deal especially in vegetables. The present buildings were put up by the Corporation of London and opened in 1928 as a 'fruit and veg' market with special heated cellars for ripening bananas. The area has an intensely rich cultural history and has seen waves of immigrants who brought distinctive trades and traditions with them – the Huguenots, expelled from France in 1685, Jews in the 19th century and Bangladeshis (of Brick Lane fame) in the 20th. The current licensee, Sandra Esquilant, is of Huguenot descent.

TEN BELLS ❷

84 Commercial Street, Spitalfields, E1 6LY
020 7366 1721
Grade II listed.
Tube and railway station: Liverpool Street.
Real ale.

A four-storey corner pub, right opposite the magnificent Christ Church, Spitalfields and Spitalfields Market. The outside could do with a little sprucing up but at least it retains the insignia of the former owners, the major brewers, Truman, Hanbury and Buxton who operated from Brick Lane nearby.

The interior has been gutted to make a smart bar but the pub is included here for its wall tiling of around 1900. On the left, just inside what would have been an entrance corridor, is a tiled mural entitled 'Spitalfields in ye Olden Time – Visiting a Weaver's Shop'. Here we have a prosperous-looking lady and gent (complete with young black servant) surrounded by deferential locals, inspecting a piece of cloth. Spitalfields was a centre of the silk-weaving industry established by Huguenots. The mural is signed 'W B Simpson & Sons. 100. S. Martins Lane. LONDON'. Simpson's were responsible for a great many tiling schemes in pubs a century or so ago. Otherwise there are large tiled panels with swirling blue and white Arabesque decoration.

History across the road: Over the road from the pub is the towering presence of Christ Church, Spitalfields, one of the great churches of the 18th century. The magnificent design was by Nicholas Hawksmoor and the church was put up it 1714-29.

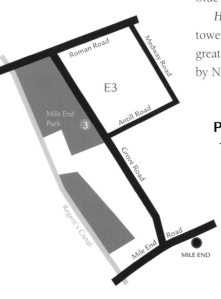

MAP: E3

PALM TREE ❸

127 Grove Road, Bow, E3 5BH
020 8980 2918
Not listed.
Tube: Mile End.
Real ale.

A rebuild by Truman's in the 1930s. With the surrounding housing vanished, thanks first to Hitler and then the even more energetic post-war planners, it looks strangely adrift in a green area beside the Regent's Canal.

The exterior has buff and mottled grey-blue ceramic work and also displays Truman's proud eagle. Inside there are still two completely separate rooms. The corner one was originally further subdivided into two. It has a particularly attractive sweeping hemispherical end to the bar counter. The other room was intended to be the smarter area of the pub as can be seen by the rather finer detailing of the counter (panelled as opposed to upright tongue-and-grooved work). Both counters have before them the typical Truman's tiled chequerwork and both also have openings for access to the beer engines. On the right-hand side it looks as though the dart board cover might be a survivor from the 1930s. The pub's loos all have their original tilework (apart from the gents' off the corner bar). The loose furniture is worth a look for some attractive benches on the right-hand side and the 1930s tables in both bars. Those in the corner bar have unusual cork tops, as does the counter on the right-hand side.

History close by: The canal was begun in 1812 to connect the Grand Union Canal at Paddington Basin with the Thames at Limehouse. Two tunnels, forty bridges, twelve locks and eight years later it opened to become a major stimulus to commerce.

Above: **Palm Tree exterior**

Below: **Palm Tree interior with 1930s tables**

ELDERFIELD
(formerly Priory Tavern, then Eclipse) ❹
57 Elderfield Road, Clapton, E5 0LF
020 8986 1591
Not listed.
Railway station: Homerton.
Real ale.

This three-storey Victorian corner-site pub dates back to the 1860s when the area was being developed. It was given a major makeover in about 1935 which is what forms the real interest today. The ground floor received a grey granite facing and the whole interior was refitted.

Entering from the Blurton Road side, the bar there is notable with characteristic two-thirds-height panelling and a large circular feature for concealed lighting. The counter steps forward in three stages. The bar-back and fire surround are from the same scheme but the overmantel has been altered. There are beautifully veneered doors to the loos and the lettering over is probably original. The ladies' has been refitted but the gents'

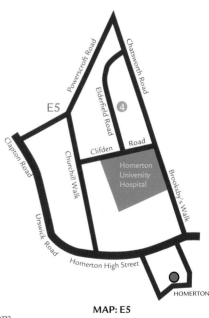

MAP: E5

Above: **Interior of the Elderfield**

has its original tiling although some TLC is perhaps needed to recapture the true spirit of the 1930s.

The other, larger bar, now accessed through a walkway, has much less of interest and is partly old – such as the bar counter and herring-bone woodblock floor – and partly new. Markings on the floor clearly show that there was once a small, separate compartment: perhaps this was an off-sales area but quite how it linked to the servery is unclear.

BOLEYN ⑤

1 Barking Road, East Ham, E6 1PW
020 8472 2182.
Grade II listed.
Tube: Upton Park.

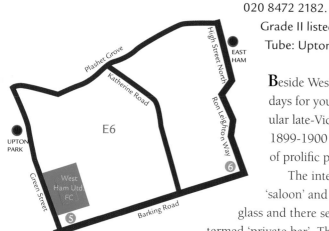

MAP: E6

Below: **Boleyn exterior**

Beside West Ham's football ground (avoid match days for your visit!), this is one of the more spectacular late-Victorian pubs in London. It was built in 1899-1900 in free Renaissance style to the designs of prolific pub architects Shoebridge & Rising.

The interior is a tour de force. The names 'saloon' and 'private bar' are preserved in the door glass and there seem to have been two or three spaces termed 'private bar'. The tiled corridor off Barking Road leads past one and there was a further, tiny one between this and the saloon behind. Over the saloon is a small skylight with lovely stained glass. Beyond lies a spectacular billiard room with a much larger stained glass skylight and a coved frieze with abundant Florentine decoration.

Other old features include the bar counter, cast-iron columns and lots of decorative glass although the servery back fitting is modern. An intriguing feature is a pair of very low doors in the stub of screening at the back of the saloon and in the screen between the saloon and private bar. Such doors allowed staff access between compartments but these are unusually low – either East Ham was populated by dwarves about 1900 or the pub relied on child labour!

History next door: West Ham United were founded in 1895 as the Thames Ironworks FC and took its present name in 1900. The club has never fallen outside the top two divisions and has won the FA Cup three times – 1964, 1975 and 1980.

DENMARK ARMS

381 Barking Road, East Ham, E6 1LA
020 8472 0535.
Grade II listed.
Tube: East Ham.

Over the crossroads from the stunning town hall, this is a pub in two parts – a late 19th-century building on the corner and a major extension of 1903 up Ron Leighton Way.

The ground floor is now one large room wrapped around the servery (modern back fittings) but what makes it special are the ornate details, notably the lovely tiled frieze on the back wall of the older part of the pub with its plain green tiles and statuesque rose bushes. Above is a mottled alabaster band then a decorative frieze with tendrils swirling round stylised rosettes.

In the new part (former saloon) the treatment is different with a ceiling divided into bold panels with deep cornices and a high-level frieze with figures. The columns in the two areas are also different – thin Corinthian ones in the older area, chunky Ionic ones in the newer.

Above: **Ornately-detailed interior of the Denmark Arms**

Below: **Denmark Arms exterior**

If the pub is not too busy do ask to see the upper floor (now a function room). The front part was a restaurant and the back almost certainly a billiard room, and a very spectacular one at that with a fine skylight and a glazed-in servery with hatches. At the foot of the stair is a unique feature for a pub – a ticket booth-style shop for selling cigarettes and drink. This looks inter-war as do many of the features of the upper floor. There is a separate, tall entrance with staircase from Ron Leighton Way.

DOLPHIN ⑦

165 Mare Street, Hackney, E8 3RH
020 8985 3727
Not listed.
Railway station: London Fields.
NI Part Two.
Opens at 1pm (closes after midnight).

The exterior of this pub belies the riches within. Much has changed since around 1900 when it was refitted but the wall tiling is a very special survival. It is by W B Simpson & Sons who tiled many a London pub. The star feature is the right-hand

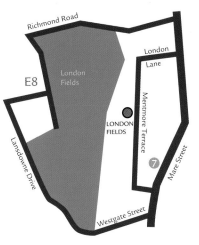

MAP: E8

BETWEEN THE WARS

By the 1920s there was a strong reaction against all things Victorian and this definitely included glittery-looking pubs. Inter-war pubs still retained a hierarchical distinction of rooms but the architecture and fittings were much more restrained than their Victorian counterparts. Yet nostalgia (as today) was still part of the notion of the pub. A popular vehicle for this was through 'brewers' Tudor' – lots of external half-timbering, beamed ceilings inside, plenty of panelling, even perhaps a baronial-style hall as at the Windsor Castle, Battersea (p178), and the

Black glass advertising panel at the Forest Hill Tavern – see Herne Tavern (p156)

Elegant, restrained 1930s fittings at the Lord Derby, Plumstead (p153) at Christmas time

'Oak Room' at the Eastbrook, Dagenham (p137). Plain and respectable neo-Georgian architecture with unostentatious fittingsand a good deal of wall panelling were very popular indeed. Sadly Art Deco – that seductive style of seaside lidos and Odeon cinemas with its streamlining, sleek surfaces and clean geometry – is poorly represented in London pubs. The best examples, perhaps, are the interior of the Duke of York, Bloomsbury (p10), and

the private bar at the Doctor Johnson, Barkingside (p133). Occasionally 1930s loose furniture survives: good, distinctive examples can be found at the Fox & Pheasant, West Brompton (p176), the Herne Tavern, East Dulwich (p156) and the Palm Tree, Bow (p120).

Truman, Hanbury, Buxton & Co. were one of the major London brewers whose Black Eagle Brewery was in Brick Lane, Stepney. After a history stretching back to 1666, they were taken over in 1974 by Watneys who closed them down fifteen years later. Their emblem, the black eagle, still adorns many a pub in east and central London. Truman's rebuilding and refitting schemes are usually of some distinction and produced a number of interiors of note. Pleasing examples to visit are the Golden Heart, Spitalfields (p119), Rose & Crown, Stoke Newington (pp113) and the Duke of Edinburgh, Brixton (p175). There is a distinct Truman's house style characterised by elegant, light-coloured wall-panelling (frequently with gold lettering at the top advertising their wares), simple linear bar-back fittings, attractive brick or tiled fireplaces, and chequerwork tilework in front of some of the counters which was often used to create a spittoon trough.

Typical Truman's advertising on woodwork at the Duke of Edinburgh, Brixton (p173)

wall which lined a former corridor (the footprint of the corridor can still be easily seen). There are blue and white tiles with pairs of birds and swirling Arabesque patterns but near the entrance is a vast tile panel depicting the legend of Arion. He is thought to have lived in about 600BC and the legend goes that on his return from a profitable trip to Italy and Sicily it was his misfortune to be be thrown overboard by avaricious sailors. Luckily for him a friendly dolphin was on hand to carry him safely to land, as narrated in the inscription.

Above: **Decorative tile panel inside the Dolphin**

On the other side of the pub an entrance panel depicts Diana the Huntress; then come more blue and white bird-and-foliage panels. As for the other fittings, the counter is largely of c.1900, as is the central stillion. There is a separate room at the rear-left although its panelling seems modern. Other remaining screenwork shows how the front part of the pub would have been divided into separate drinking spaces.

COLEGRAVE ARMS ⑧

145 Cann Hall Road, Leytonstone, E11 3NJ
020 8522 0184
Not listed.
Railway Station: Leytonstone High Road.
Real ale.

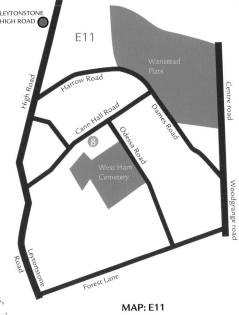

MAP: E11

This Victorian corner-site Charrington's pub was given a thorough, if rather plain, refit in the 1930s. The mottled beige tiling applied to the ground floor exterior is still there behind a layer of paint that someone has short-sightedly applied. Inside, the work fares better with three separate rooms still with their 1930s fittings.

At the front lie the public bar and a smaller snug, both accessed from a common, promontory servery. This has a central fitting with plain mirrors in the panels, and attractive lettering at the top advertising Charrington's wares – Toby Ale and Toby Stout (Charrington's emblem was a Toby jug). The snug is the most intimate part of the pub and is nicely fitted out, as is the public bar, with wall panelling decorated with concave vertical strips.

At the rear is a large lounge, much bigger than the front area. The servery extends back into it and the Charrington's advertising reappears with the blandishments of 'wines and spirits'

and 'barley wine'. The walls are divided up by wooden strips into large vertical panels.

History in a name: The pub derives its names from the Colegraves who bought the manor in 1671. They continued to hold Cann Hall as a country estate until the early 19th century. Most of the estate was sold for development in 1880-95 though the family retained part of it until 1900.

EARL OF ESSEX ⑨

616 Romford Road, Manor Park, E12 5AF
020 8553 5164
Grade II listed.
Railway Station: Woodgrange Park.

An imposing Edwardian corner pub of 1902 by architects W E Trent and Henry Poston for one Joseph Hill. It is a lavish architectural display with a corner turret and a couple of first-floor balconies. Though rather dilapidated, it retains three distinct areas gathered round a central servery. The large room fronting High Street North is split by a timber and glass screen but originally it would have been further subdivided – see the multiple doors from the rather grand, mosaic-floored entrance and the changes in bar counter design

The least-altered part is the delightful private bar off Romford Road – currently used for storage but retaining its fittings, even down to a glazed display cabinet. Behind comes a large, dark area, probably once a billiard room, with a blocked skylight and deep cornice.

The original servery fittings include an unusual bar-back with sub-Jacobean detail, built-in clock and mirrored panels. There is also good ceiling decoration, a little etched glass and three very striking fireplaces. These latter break with the tradition of ornate Victorian or Edwardian work and their clean lines would not be out of place in a building 25 years later.

History in a name: It's not exactly clear which Earl of Essex is commemorated here but most likely Robert Devereux, a favourite of Elizabeth I. He undertook various military expeditions including the storming of Cadiz in 1596 but fell out of favour after a disastrous expedition against Ireland in 1599. He went on to plot against the Queen and, in consequence, he and his head parted company in 1601.

<< LEFT HAND PAGE

Edwardian interior of the Earl of Essex

MAP: E12

Below: **Earl of Essex's imposing Edwardian frontage**

MODERN TIMES – THE CHANGING APPEARANCE OF PUBS

There was hardly any pub building or refitting during the first ten years that followed the economically devastating World War II. From the mid-fifties, when things started to get going again, material shortages and the tough economic environment meant that things had to be done on the cheap but otherwise it is often not easy to distinguish between work of 1939 or 1959. But that was about to change dramatically.

By far the most important change affecting the fabric of our pubs over the past forty years or so has been opening out. Social segregation in the pub became far less important, thus removing the need for a basic public bar and a smarter room or rooms. You find many a Victorian London pub with its old counter sitting like an island or a peninsula surrounded by a single drinking space. The old partitions have all been swept away and you can often trace how many there would have been by the number of external doors, each of which would have led to its own individual drinking area.

Another major change has been the demise of the jug and bottle (or off-sales) department where people used to buy take-home supplies. Changes to rules governing the sale in supermarkets in the early 1960s led to a huge shake up in how and where we buy our alcohol so we now buy our drink from Tesco rather than the Red Lion. Some redundant off-sales compartments do survive but, not surprisingly, many have been knocked into an adjacent on-sales drinking space.

Early 20th-century pubgoers expected a degree of privacy from the outside world and they got it by means of etched or patterned window glass. The last couple of decades have seen a significant tendency to replace this with plain glazing. This is usually put down to making pubs more 'women-friendly' but the price has been the loss of massive amounts of magnificent Victorian glass. This was intended to create a translucent veil between the glamorous world of the pub and the mundane world outside and at night, especially, it creates a wonderful effect.

And on a final curmudgeonly note – bar counters. Have you ever noticed how so many of them look an utter mess! Old pictures show that down to the 1950s counters were unencumbered affairs with some hand-pumps and perhaps, say, a display cabinet for sandwiches, pies etc. Even pot-shelves (the common name for those gantry-like structures standing on counters) were rare. Sadly this is not the case today and the latter are usually quite ugly and form an unfriendly, fortress-like barrier between staff and customers. The arrival of lagers, smoothflow beers, keg cider and stout etc. has also led to a multiplicity of tall fonts of all sorts, doing the appearance of pubs no favours at all.

Garish keg fonts compete with traditional handpumps at the King's Head, Tooting (p186)

GEORGE ⑩

114 Glengall Grove, Isle of Dogs, E14 3ND
020 7987 2954
Not listed.
DLR: Crossharbour & London Arena.
Real ale.

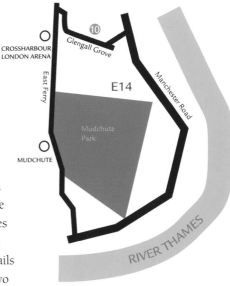

MAP: E14

The George was rebuilt in a rather austere, red-brick neo-Georgian style about 1930 and has kept three separate rooms and many original fittings. The best room is the left-hand one on the long façade. This has extensive panelling, the original bar counter and fittings and a series of pretty plaster friezes decorated with what appear to be blackberries and dog roses. There are a few Art Deco details scattered around, as for example on the fire surround. Two openings lead to a modern conservatory dining area.

The next room is a small snug entirely separated from the previous one and again has various fittings from about 1930. A door leads on to the corner bar, the most interesting feature of which is a bar counter with hefty, lapped boards to the front. This area has incorporated an off-sales area, detectable in a blocked doorway, which is visible outside. Most of the panelling in this room is relatively modern wood and is, unfortunately, rather cheaply done.

History round about: The Isle of Dogs is the promontory of land formed by a loop in the Thames opposite Greenwich. Not an island originally, the name (obscure in itself) is taken from a long-vanished island in the river. It was farmland until the northern part became the site of the West India Docks (opened 1802). Then in 1805 a canal was cut across the top of the peninsula so that at last the Isle of Dogs became an island.

Above: **George, 1930s exterior**
Below: **George interior**

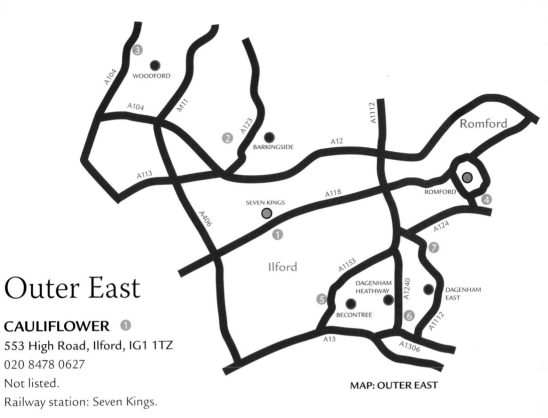

MAP: OUTER EAST

Outer East

CAULIFLOWER ❶

553 High Road, Ilford, IG1 1TZ

020 8478 0627

Not listed.

Railway station: Seven Kings.

A vast edifice, some way out of the centre, on the main road east out of Ilford. It dates from the great pub boom around 1900 and still has the vestiges of a truly wonderful interior. The imposing frontage is more or less symmetrical and, stylistically, is a revival of architecture from around 1600.

The interior has been largely opened out but immediately by the main entrance is a screen with a wide round arch in a timber and glass surround which provides some kind of subdivision in the front part of the pub. The servery is large and caters to all parts of the pub. In the middle it has an ornate stillion stretching right up to the high, decorated ceiling and incorporating a built-in clock and a lovely small, glazed-in office. The counter curves round in an L-shape at the back and carries a couple of brass water dispensers for diluting spirits. The stillion and right-hand side wall of the rear area have splendid etched and polished glass while one of two skylights survives at the rear (though now with horrid modern glass and boarded over). A couple of 'original' features that might trick the unwary – the little drinking alcoves on the left have been created out of a former corridor and the bell-pushes at the rear (and indicator box in the stillion) probably date from around 1960-80.

<< LEFT HAND PAGE

Tiled floor inside the Cauliflower

DOCTOR JOHNSON ❷

Longwood Gardens (corner of Rushden Gardens),
Barkingside, IG5 0ES
020 8550 0497
Grade II listed.
NI Part One.
Real ale.

One of the best examples anywhere to show how a typical, large, 1930s housing estate pub might have looked. It is in the popular, loosely neo-Georgian style combined with 1930s Art Deco streamlining – hence the broad curve which turns the corner from one elevation to the other. The Doctor Johnson opened in 1938 and was designed by the architect H Reginald Ross for Courage, one of whose directors was an enthusiast of the great lexicographer. Johnson himself appears high up on each elevation in bas-relief portraits by artist Arthur Betts.

Architecturally the pub is not at all unusual for its time but what makes it special is the survival of the internal layout, four rooms, each with its own bar counter, ranged around the central serving area. On the corner is the quadrant-shaped snug with Art Deco details. Left is the large public bar and right comes the saloon. Behind is a vast lounge which gives on to the garden. There are many original features to look out for such as the curvy Art Deco cornices in the snug and public bar, the fireplaces with their upright tiled decoration in the same rooms, the remnants of the revolving door to the saloon and the incised and colour vertical lettering to loo doors.

Note the estate agent's office on the left-hand side of the pub. This was originally an off-licence linked to the pub cellar by a below-ground passage.

Above: **Curved exterior of the Doctor Johnson**
Below: **Doctor Johnson loo signs**

<< *LEFT HAND PAGE*
Art Deco private bar at the Doctor Johnson

TRAVELLERS FRIEND ❸

496-8 High Road, Woodford Green, IG8 0PN
020 8504 2435
Tube: Woodford.
Real ale.

Below: **Interior of Travellers Friend**

A delightful, small, no-nonsense pub situated in an early 19th-century three-storey building on the main road out of Woodford Green heading for Epping Forest. It is said to have been licensed

Above: **Drinkers enjoy a pint outside the Travellers Friend**

for beer and port sales in 1832. Outside is a fine, curly bracket for the pub lantern. Inside, three bars have been combined into one forming a U-shape round the servery and the stairs up to the living accommodation.

The plain, boarded counter and the bar-back are hard to date and, parts at least, may be earlier than the inter-war remodelling that lends the pub its main character. The latter involves fielded panelling along the side and back walls and brick fireplaces on either side. The revamp may date from a time when a full licence was granted. Note the four stubs in the left-hand part of the bar-back which are the relics from taps said to have served port by gravity from casks overhead. A further feature of interest is the bank of five snob screens on the left-hand side of the bar counter. They cannot be in situ since the counter front below has evidence of former access to the serving area. There is modern etched glass in the front windows. The counter has a panel which could be removed to allow for servicing the beer engines in former times.

History in the area: North-west of the pub is an area called Woodford Wells where the water from the local springs was used for medicinal purposes.

Above: **Exterior of the Wheatsheaf**

Below: **Wheatsheaf interior**

WHEATSHEAF

45 Wheatsheaf Road, Romford, RM1 2HD
01708 736934
Railway station: Romford.
Real ale.

A little way to the south of the centre of Romford, the Wheatsheaf is a rebuild of about 1930 to serve a rather drab housing estate. The exterior has a little imitation half-timbering on the upper floors to create the then-popular Tudor effect. There is a pretty timber verandah on the front which used to give access to a now-vanished enclosed outside seating area.

There are still two totally separated rooms, a public bar on the left and a small saloon to the right. The public bar has not only taken in the jug and bottle but also involved the amalgamation of two other rooms and is now a large U-shaped space. The panelling is simple but original to the building, as are the bar counter, back fitting and exposed, applied wooden strips on the ceiling. Note the dumb waiter on the left-hand side of the servery. The woodwork in the saloon is similar in style to that next door and creates a most attractive, intimate room. The fire surround is original but the tiled insert is recent.

ROUNDHOUSE ⑤

Lodge Avenue, Becontree, Dagenham, RM8 2HY
020 8592 1605
Not listed.
Tube: Becontree.

This daunting pub near the western edge of the vast Becontree Estate was built in 1936. It has a most unusual design, the work of specialist pub architect, Alfred W Blomfield. As the name suggests the ground plan is round and on top of this there sits a T-shaped upper storey with a bulky square tower in the centre.

This is a classic example of the large inter-war pubs that went up on housing estates to serve great swathes of housing and provide extensive facilities – and not just for alcohol drinkers. This one had a tea room and a wing containing an indoor bowling green. Blomfield also provided a huge oval lounge at

Above: **Roundhouse interior**

Below: **Circular exterior of the Roundhouse**

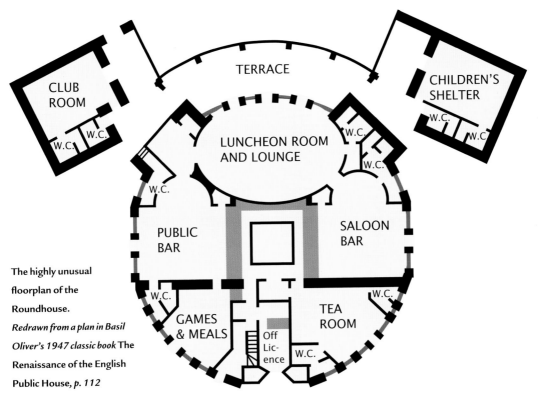

The highly unusual floorplan of the Roundhouse.

Redrawn from a plan in Basil Oliver's 1947 classic book The Renaissance of the English Public House, *p. 112*

the rear and this still survives but with a cut-through to the adjacent room at the front. This in turn is separated by a wall from the rest of the pub where one can still get some sense of the original spaces. The fittings, apart from some sub-Art Deco wall panelling, are largely replacements.

History nearby: the Becontree Estate is a phenomenon, albeit a pretty grim one. In 1919 the London County Council was allowed to build outside the old county of London and plans were drawn up to accommodate 120,000 people in 24,000 terraced houses on what was then Essex agricultural land. By 1935 the scheme was officially complete and 167,000 people had been housed. Further development took place after World War II.

ADMIRAL VERNON ⑥

141 Broad Street, Dagenham, RM10 9HP
020 8592 0431
Not listed.
Tube: Dagenham Heathway.

Above: **Brewers' Tudor exterior of the Admiral Vernon**

Below: **Admiral Vernon interior**

A 1930s estate pub which has kept a good deal of its original plan, fittings and character. It is in the popular 'brewers' Tudor' style with imitation half-timbering above and buff faïence cladding below.

On the far left is a former off-sales shop, now disused of course. Then comes the public bar which, like the rest of the pub, has three-quarter-height wall panelling. The vine decoration in the cornices is also repeated throughout. Beyond the main public bar is a smaller extension and the remnants of a sliding screen that would have separated the two (the rear part has a sash window to the servery). The screen on the right of the public bar has a low service doorway to what was a snug. This has now been amalgamated with the saloon. Further right still is a still extant sliding screen to the large rear room. The counter and back fittings are original as is the high, pink terrazzo spittoon trough which still stands in front of the counter.

History in a name: Edward Vernon (1684-1757) is an appropriate dedicatee for a pub name since he was the first to introduce grog (rum diluted with water) for his sailors in 1740 when a captain in the West Indies. He was promoted to admiral in 1745, but attacked the Admiralty in a series of anonymous pamphlets in 1745-6 and was cashiered in 1746.

EASTBROOK

Dagenham Road, Dagenham, RM10 7UP
020 8592 1873
Not listed.
Tube: Dagenham East.
NI Part One.
Real ale.

Above: **Stained glass windows in the Eastbrook**

Below: **Eastbrook 1930s interior**

For quality and completeness this is the finest 1930s pub in this book and, indeed, one of the best anywhere. It was built in 1937 for G A Smith & Sons, wine merchants and off-sales proprietors, whose name is still in evidence, notably on the still-functioning adjacent off-licence. The architecture makes considerable play of panels of brick alternating with render, and hipped roofs with pantile coverings. The left-hand projection (explained inside) makes the building decidedly asymmetrical.

There are two separate bars known as the Oak Room (right) and the Walnut Room (centre) plus the left-hand projection which was called the Music Room – hence the stained glass depicting a variety of instruments and framed by wooden Tuscan columns. The room size can be varied by a folding glazed screen. There is another such screen to the elegant Walnut Room, named for the wood used for the counter (note its distinctive circular decoration) and the high-level screen above. Don't miss the Art Deco-style mirrors in the bar-back with their wavy decoration. More columns frame the front area.

The Oak Room (so-called for obvious reasons) is plainer and played public bar to the Walnut's saloon. Here the style is 'brewers' Tudor'. So we have beams cased in to imitate sturdy timbers, exposed joists, Tudor arches in the servery area and much wall panelling. The counter and bar-back fittings are original but perhaps the most remarkable survivors are the half dozen glass and metal light fittings. In all, this is a truly remarkable survivor which will repay the trek out to see it.

History in the area: The nearby Sterling Industrial Estate takes its name from Dagenham's Sterling Armament Company where the Sterling submachine gun was manufactured in the 20th century.

Right: **Courtyard of the George, an old galleried coaching inn**

Below: **George interior**

SOUTH EAST

SE1 to SE28

GEORGE ❶

77 Borough High Street, Borough, SE1 1NH
020 7407 2056.
Grade I listed.
Tube and railway station: London Bridge.
NI Part Two.
Real ale.

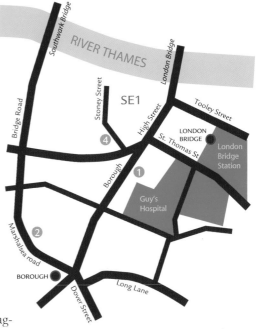

MAP: SE1 (PART 1)

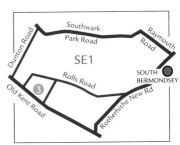

MAP: SE1 (PART 2)

An amazing survivor from the days when Southwark was a major terminus for the coaching trade between London and southern England. The George was rebuilt in 1676 after a major fire in Southwark and is the last galleried coaching inn in London – but even this is but a fragment of its former self. It used to extend round the four sides of a courtyard – just as the New Inn in Gloucester does to this day. Part of it was demolished in 1889 to make way for the construction of the railway.

Most of the pub's spaces involve modern fittings but the first bar you come to has some of the oldest woodwork purpose-fitted for a pub anywhere (some of it might even date back to the rebuilding of the inn). It was evidently two rooms at one time but they have been amalgamated. In the part nearest the road is full-height horizontal boarding and simple fixed seating against the walls and in the window. There is an ancient fireplace with a wooden hood and a clock that reminded travellers of the time.

The larger part of this room has a mighty fireplace and a glazed-in servery with vertical sashes. Inside you can see a now-disused set of 'cash-register'-style Victorian hand pumps (the handles move in quadrant-shaped slots to draw the beer). Their maker's name – South of Blackfriars Road – is prominently in evidence.

Near by: You may also care to visit the Shipwrights' Arms, 88 Tooley Street, where you will find a splendid painted tiled panel of around 1900 in a former entrance lobby showing shipwrights at work and traffic on the river.

History in the area: Southwark lies astride the ancient approach to and from London across London Bridge. It was famous for its numerous inns which included the Tabard from where Chaucer's 14th-century pilgrims set out for their trip to Canterbury. The vanished White Hart appeared both in Shakespeare's *Henry VI* and Dickens's *Pickwick Papers* while the also-demolished Queen's Head provided John Harvard with the means for setting up Harvard University. Southwark was a major centre for hop trading, a reminder of which is the splendid façade of 1866 of the Hop Exchange on Southwark Street.

LORD CLYDE ❷

27 Clennam Street, Borough, SE1 1ER
020 7407 3397
Not listed.
Tube: Borough.
Real ale.

In what must be the shortest street in London, the delightful Lord Clyde pub was rebuilt in 1913 and has a marvellous exterior with lots of ceramic work. Pride of place goes to a majestic eagle, the emblem of East End brewers, Truman, Hanbury and Buxton, while the fascia over the corner entrance bears the name 'E J Bayling' who must have been the owner and/or licensee on the eve of the Great War. Even the window surrounds are are highly decorative.

Above: **Tiled exterior and fascia of the Lord Clyde**

Below: **Lord Clyde interior**

Inside, there are two rooms. The public bar (front) has a tapering, matchboarded counter and partly panelled walls. Note the fine mirror advertising 'Mild Ales and Dublin Stout'. The back bar has a hatch to the servery and more wall panelling. A framed Truman's price list tells us the prices of beer back in 1961. The fittings and detailing have a restraint and simplicity which forms a marked contrast to the ornateness of pubs from a decade or so before and gives a hint of what would come after the First World War.

History in a name: Colin Campbell Clyde was a distinguished Victorian commander who was granted a peerage in 1858 for his part in putting down the Indian Mutiny the previous year.

History in the area: The notorious debtors' prison, the Marshalsea, was near Mermaid Court off Borough High Street. It was rebuilt on Borough High Street and opened in 1811.

Charles Dickens' father was imprisoned there and Dickens' masterpieces *David Copperfield* and *Little Dorrit* both feature episodes set in the prison. It closed in 1842 after an Act of Parliament resulted in fewer people being imprisoned for debt. In 1849 most of the building was demolished but parts were converted in the 20th century and became a printworks. These, in turn, were demolished in the 1970s and replaced by two municipal buildings, the John Harvard Library and the Local Studies Library.

LORD NELSON ③

386 Old Kent Road, Bermondsey, SE1 5AA
020 7701 8510
Grade II listed.
Railway station: South Bermondsey.

Above: **Lord Nelson interior**
Below: **Lord Nelson, Cape Vincent**
mirror detail

The Lord Nelson was once magnificent – even now it retains some of the most spectacular mirrorwork in the country. Pride of place goes to a large painted and gilded mirror of the great admiral receiving the surrender after the battle of Cape Vincent in 1797 from some shifty, swarthy Spanish types. There are two more vast mirrors behind the servery but one is cracked and the other is largely covered up. The maker was a James Carter of Gray's Inn Road and they date from around 1888. The details include grapes, kingfishers, vases of fruit and foliage trails.

There is also what is probably a unique feature in a pub – an impressive timber arcade striding across the servery with two bays sitting on top of the counter and a third spanning a walkway between two counters. The screen and bar-back have wonderful detail including coloured panels advertising all manner of drinks – champagne, finest old brandies, liqueurs, ports and sherries – the list goes on.

The serving area has an extraordinary shape and projects out into the main bar. This is because it serviced a whole variety of small compartments, reminders of which are preserved in the door glass (perhaps of the 1950s), which notes 'public bar' and 'saloon bar'. At the rear is another room entered through an archway. It too has its own outside entrance with fine Victorian decorative glass (also proclaiming 'saloon bar'). This room also has its own counter screen, like that in the main bar, which has a fine old clock situated over a doorway.

MODERN TIMES –
FROM BREWERY TO PUBCO

Time was when your local was probably owned by a brewery. Now it almost certainly isn't. By 1914 most London pubs had become tied houses owned by brewers and so things remained until the 1990s. Individual brewers had their own insignia and range of products and there was no mistaking whose house you were in – the 1930s Truman's pubs featured on pxx are good examples. Your next pub visit is likely to be to a house belonging to a pub-owning company (or 'pubco' for short) and you have no way of knowing whose it is.

In 1989, after a lengthy enquiry, the government hit upon a bright piece of legislation to safeguard consumer choice, known for short as the Beer Orders. Any brewer with a tied estate of more than 2,000 pubs was to sell off or free the tie on any pubs in excess of that number and tied landlords should be allowed to purchase a guest ale from anyone they wished. The intention was one thing, the results something very different. The big brewers promptly either split their activities into separate brewing and pub-owning companies or sold off their breweries to concentrate on what had been their tied estates, which they saw as offering the greater business opportunity. Either way, the result was the same. And the ironic thing is that two huge pubcos now own one in every four pubs in the country – Punch Taverns with over 8,400 houses, closely followed by Enterprise Inns with 7,800 (figures at January 2008). So much for stimulating competition!

We do still have one major London brewer left with traditional tied pubs. This is Fuller's of Chiswick whose estate of 360 pubs includes 145 in our area. Until late 2006 the situation was similar with Young's but, with the closure of their Wandsworth brewery and the transfer of brewing to the Charles Wells site in Bedford, they are now another pubco. The products and the styling of their houses, however, still resembles the old Young's brand: of their 213 pubs, 155 are in Greater London. The only other virtually integrated companies of significance operating in London are Greene King of Bury St Edmund's with a few dozen of their 1,600 houses in the capital, and Yorkshire brewer, Samuel Smith's, who have about 20 pubs in the Greater London area.

Fuller's of Chiswick, brewery sign

History in the area: The Old Kent Road follows the course of the Roman Watling Street running between London and Dover and was the route taken by medieval pilgrims to Canterbury. Until the end of the 19th century it was known as Kent Street Road, being a continuation of Kent Street in the Borough. More recently, in the 20th century, the area had become notorious as a haunt of criminals.

WHEATSHEAF ❹

6 Stoney Street, Borough, SE1 9AA
020 7407 7242
Grade II listed.
Tube and railway station: London Bridge.
Real ale.

In 1890 when this pub was rebuilt it was no doubt a fairly basic establishment, serving people using and serving Borough Market. Nowadays the market is massively gentrified (with prices to match!) but the Wheatsheaf still looks much as it has done for a couple of generations.

The pub stretches back from the street and is split down the middle by a screen which is straddled by the servery. The door glass helpfully informs us that the left-hand part was the public bar and the right-hand was the saloon. The sense of separation is still much in evidence though the screen has been broken through at the rear – most people frequenting this area today are pretty well-off and therefore not too bothered about social separation in their pubs.

The glass in the front windows suggests inter-war work and much of what we see inside may well date from that time. The walls have full-height matchboard panelling and the detailing of the counters and screen is quite plain. A very nice modern touch is the series of prints by Mychael Barratt, mostly 'Life Imitating Art' scenes of daily life in London incorporating references to famous paintings.

History across the road: Borough fruit and vegetable market received its charter in 1671 and originally spread over a large area but in the mid-18th century it was abolished and the present market was set up in Rochester Yard in the mid-19th century. The Borough High Street entrance dates from 1932.

Above: **Wheatsheaf exterior**

Below: **1930s interior of the Wheatsheaf**

THE DUKE OF CLARENCE

CORRIB BAR

FREE HOUSE

CORRIB BAR

The Corrib Bar

Breakfast Available
T-Bone steak & 2 veg £
Steak & 2 veg £4.95
Boiled Bacon & 2 veg £3.55
Sausages & chips
with Beans £2.50
¼ Pounder & chips with
Beans or Onions £2.50
Fish & Chips with Peas £2.50
Camberwell Special £1.70

¼ Pounder Sandwich £2.50

Sandwiches
Ham · Cheese ·
Salmon · Tuna
Boiled Bacon ·
Bacon, Lettuce & Tomato
For other fillings
please ask inside
Door step Sandwich

Tea · Coffee & Soup
Available

This Pub is now open from 10AM.

Red Bull

This Pub
IS NOW OPEN
FROM
10 AM EVERYDAY

CORRIB BAR
(formerly Duke of Clarence) ⑤

181 Camberwell Road, Camberwell, SE5 0HB
020 7703 4007
Not listed.
Tube: Oval.

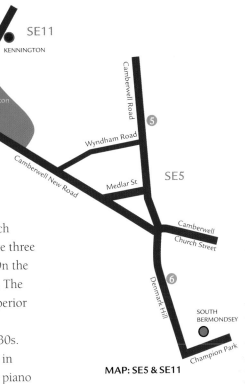

MAP: SE5 & SE11

A remarkably unaltered 1930s pub that is worth a visit to see how many smallish street-corner local pubs must have looked. It was built by East End brewers Charringtons, as indicated by their emblem of the Toby jug on the large tiled panel which bears the former pub name in diagonal lettering. There are three rooms ranged along the side street, New Church Road. On the corner is the public bar, then a snug and finally a saloon. The higher status of the saloon is indicated by the slightly superior panelling compared with the other two rooms.

The fittings are all low-key as was common in the 1930s. The most striking feature perhaps is the band of terrazzo in front of the snug bar counter, patterned like an over-size piano keyboard. The bar-back has unusual treatment with dimpled glass panels forming the back wall to it and the front windows too have some surviving dimpled glazing and strips of green glass.

History on the spot: This pub was patronised by the notorious 1960s Richardson gang whose leader, Charlie, had his scrapyard close by. He and his brother Eddie led a life of theft, fraud, extortion, handling stolen goods and were infamous for torturing those who crossed them or whose loyalty was suspect. They feuded with the East End Krays and were arrested in 1966.

<< *LEFT HAND PAGE*
Corrib Bar red-brick exterior

Below: **Corrib Bar tile detail**
Bottom: **Corrib Bar interior**

JOINERS' ARMS ⑥

35 Denmark Hill, Camberwell, SE5 8RS
020 7703 4756
Not listed.
Railway station: Denmark Hill.
Real ale.

Right in the busy centre of Camberwell, this pub, although much altered, is interesting for a couple of reasons. The first and most spectacular is the tiling on the wall of the front bar with the large panel bearing the arms of the Joiners' & Ceilers'

Above: **Joiners' Arms tile detail**

RIGHT HAND PAGE >>

'Join Truth with Trust' motto in the Joiners' Arms

Below: **Old Red Lion interior**

Company, one of some 100 City livery companies. In the outer corners of this panel are implements of the joiners' trade.

The tilework looks like the work of about 1900 but the extensive wooden fittings may be later, perhaps even of the 1920s. There is a counter to both front and back rooms of the pub, which are divided by a timber and glass screen. The counter front itself is quite plain with upright tongue-and-grooved boarding and simply detailed pilasters between the bays. At the back of the servery is a glazed-in office area.

History in the tiles: The Joiners' & Ceilers' Company was formed in 1375 and is ranked 41st in the table of precedence among livery companies, under a scheme drawn up by the City Court of Aldermen in 1514. The arms incorporate implements of the joiners' trade. The supporters are a pair of youths, naked apart from carefully positioned leafy garlands. Below the shield we can read the uplifting motto 'Join Truth with Trust'. This is rather curious since the motto of the company is actually 'Join Loyalty and Liberty' and has been so since 1769. Some artistic licence going on here!

OLD RED LION

42-4 Kennington Park Road, Kennington, SE11 4RS
020 7735 3529
Grade II listed.
Tube: Kennington.
NI Part One.
Real ale.

This local drinkers' pub is as impressive and intact an example of 'brewers' Tudor' as you will find anywhere. It was rebuilt about 1929 by London brewers, Charrington's. The outside has a display of half-timbering which gives the viewer the feel of what to expect inside.

Rather like the Wheatsheaf in Borough (p143), the pub stretches back from the road and is split down the middle by a dividing wall with the servery sitting in the middle with access to both sides. There are masses of heavy timbering, most of it with adze marks to create a sense of antiquity. There are two low, narrow doorways at each end of the servery giving access from one side of the pub to the other; over one doorway a Toby jug (the emblem of Charrington's); over the other a red lion.

60 YEARS AGO

Just before the World War II, the journalist and broadcaster, Maurice Gorham, took an affectionate look at one of his favourite institutions – the London pub. The resulting book, *The Local,* published in 1939, is a classic of pub literature and was accompanied with lithographs by Gorham's artist friend and fellow pub visitor, Edward Ardizzone. The book was reissued in 1949 as *Back to the Local,* updated to take account of the impact of the War on the pubs of the capital, with Ardizzone's colourful lithographs replaced by line drawings, reflecting post-war austerity. It presents us with an eloquent picture of what pubs were like then and brings into sharp relief many of the changes that have happened since.

Owing to shortages in a Britain impoverished by war, the beer sometimes ran out on Gorham and pubs often closed early in consequence. Certainly there was no drinking in the middle of the afternoon as that was prohibited by law. Apart from a few small, single-room pubs which are mentioned as exceptions, Gorham had a choice of setting within the pub and usually opted, as a respectable middle-class type, for a better room like the saloon or, what he identified as a still smarter version, the saloon lounge (or lounge for short). Between the public bar and the saloon in status was the private bar but, Gorham noted, it was 'tending to disappear'. Where it did exist, it was 'apt to deputise for the Ladies' Bar'. Yes, in 1949 it was still politically correct to have bars for men and bars for women.

Gorham paid a little more for his beer than users of the public bar, the 'most plebeian part of the house' where 'you can bring your lunch with you and eat it without undue comment'. Public bar regulars, however, were sometimes distrustful of those not dressed as a labourer and found their presence on the low side of the pub as a matter of 'curiosity or parsimony.' The public bar was usually the place where darts – more popular then than today – was played, boosted by the efforts of the king and queen to throw darts at a social club in Slough in 1937.

And finally the drinks. Gorham noted that in public bars '"a pint" without qualification means a pint of mild', a style of beer now all but vanished from the London scene. So too have cider-houses of which there were still a handful back in 1949. As for lager, said Gorham, 'is not a very popular drink in pubs, except in Saloon Bars during very hot weather.' How times change! What will the next 60 years have in store for our pubs?

A jug and bottle compartment in action (complete with patient customer) as pictured by Edward Ardizzone. Note the pair of snob screens

Other things to enjoy are (left) the built-in picture of Bonnie Prince Charlie landing in 1745 and (left and right) original light fittings, brick pillars and mock-heraldic cartouches of the red lion and Toby jug over the fireplaces. And finally don't miss the original tiling in the loos.

Attached to the left of the building is a feature sometimes found at inter-war pubs, a separate off-sales shop.

GLENGALL TAVERN ⑧

1 Bird in Bush Road, Peckham, SE15 6RN

020 7639 1469

Not listed.

Railway station: Queen's Road Peckham.

A visually striking community local at the west end of Bird in Bush Road on the corner of Peckham Hill Street. It went up between the wars and brings into play so many typical themes of inter-war pub building. The main one is 'brewers' Tudor' so here we have lots of mock half-timbering on the first floor and corner gable giving the 'olde Englishe' look. On the ground floor is buff tile facing, again popular for pubs around 1930 but which, in its sleekness, is almost a contradiction to the nostalgic 'brewers' Tudor' effects. Set in the roof is a series of big dormer windows.

What really counts here is the interior with its three separate rooms, still panelled up to two-thirds of the wall height. The bar counter is original too with a slightly raked front and plain panelling. There is also a low service door in the screen between two of the divisions, original ends to the fixed seating in the two smaller rooms and original glass in some of the windows.

IVY HOUSE (formerly Stuart Arms) ⑨

40 Stuart Road, Nunhead, SE15 3BE

020 7732 0222

Not listed.

Railway station: Brockley.

This pub has seen better, more prosperous days and this is reflected in the fact that the right-hand part has now been hived off for residential accommodation. It must have been enormous when originally built in the 1930s by Truman's brewery.

MAP: SE15

Above: **Glengall Tavern interior**

Below: **1930s exterior**

Above: **Ivy House Art Deco exterior**

Below: **Ivy House interior**

They have provided an unusual piece of architecture here – quite blocky with the central three bays rising to an extra floor above the side ones.

The pub is still large with two epic rooms at the back. These have interestingly contrasted characters: that on the right has a Tudor look with an inglenook fireplace, panelled walls, wood-look beams and cartouches on the walls with such would-be antique emblems as a vizored knight, a portcullis, a swan and red roses. The other room has decidedly simple Art Deco details. The front room – small in comparison – was originally no doubt intended to be a smart one as is suggested by the elegant canopy over the bar counter. The counters throughout are original but the back fittings are largely modern.

Other features to look out for are the brown and white spittoon trough tiling (a feature of many 1930s Truman's pubs) and original tiling in the gents'.

MAN OF KENT ⑩

2 Nunhead Green, Peckham, SE15 3QF
020 7639 7485
Not listed.
Railway station: Nunhead.

Below: **Coloured glazing in the Man of Kent**

This basic local is one of many pubs rebuilt by London brewer, Truman's, between the wars (see their eagle emblem high up on the building). It seems to date from the 1930s and was designed in a (loosely) neo-Georgian style. It has the faïence facing on the ground floor that was so popular at the time.

Paradoxically the interest of the interior lies in its modesty. This guide has many ornate and well crafted interiors. These have had greater chances of survival than simpler schemes which were run up on the cheap and that's exactly what we have here. The wall panelling is utilitarian ply and the bar counter is very similar although there is a band near the top imitating a more luxurious veneer.

Much of the original layout can still be discerned with an L-shaped serving area with two rooms forming an L-shape on the roadsides and a square room behind (now used for games). The former has a counter for service, the latter a hatch. Other original features are the pretty coloured glazing in the windows, doors in the bar counter and no doubt some of the loose chairs.

A more modern (perhaps1970s) curiosity is the raked bar stools which look as though they ought to defy gravity. A modern travesty (it has to be said) is the louvred screenwork at the bottom of the windows, cheaply made and producing a gloomy sense of secrecy which was never the intention of 1930s pub builders.

History nearby: Nunhead Cemetery, one of the great ring of Victorian cemeteries around London, was opened in 1840. After several years of vandalism and neglect it closed in 1969 but. under an Act of Parliament in 1975, Southwark Borough Council took it over and began restoring it. In April 1980 it reopened for burials.

ALBION ⑪

20 Albion Street, Rotherhithe, SE16 7JQ
020 7237 0182
Not listed.
Tube: Canada Water, Rotherhithe.
Real ale.

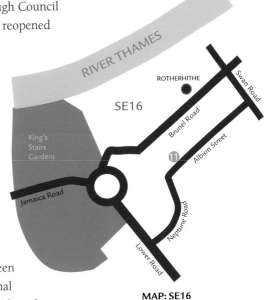

MAP: SE16

Built probably in the late 1920s this is a locals' community pub in 'brewers' Tudor' style for an inter-war estate. The ground floor tiling has, sadly, been painted over but the upper floors are in their original condition with imitation half-timbering and red brickwork.

The interior is surprisingly well preserved and retains separate rooms. On the corner is the public bar (named as such in the door glass). Behind it comes another small room which has now been opened up to the large room on the left. This looks as though it ought to have had a partition running across it but there is no evidence in the form of grooves for shutters, hinges or similar. The Albion has two-thirds-height panelling throughout of the type that was so popular between the wars. The raked counter is original and so is the woodwork in the central serving area. There are typical inter-war brick fireplaces. There are also a few jarring notes throughout such as the ironwork pot-shelves and a refrigerated food counter but all in all this is a good survival among inter-war pubs.

Also you may care to drop in at the Mayflower which fronts onto the Thames – it has some old panelling but most of the woodwork is of no great age. It is right by Brunels' Thames

Above: **Albion 1930s exterior**

HOW DISTINCTIVE ARE LONDON'S HISTORIC PUBS?

Regional differences certainly exist between urban pubs in various parts of England and Wales but they are not as strong as is sometimes supposed. Most of the pubs in this guide would be equally well at home in Birmingham, Cardiff, Exeter or Middlesbrough. But not all.

The strongest local feature of London pubs, at least around the end of the 19th century, is compartmentalisation. The capital's Victorian drinkers seemed keen on small drinking spaces to an extent unknown elsewhere in the country.

Central London is also unrivalled for the sheer concentration of rich Victorian pub artwork – glass, tiles, plasterwork and carved wood. Birmingham has its Bartons Arms, Liverpool the Philharmonic and the Vines, Belfast the Crown, and Cardiff the Golden Cross, but even allowing for its much greater size London is particularly well blessed. A tour of central London taking in (and this list is not exhaustive!) the Red Lion, St James's (p167); the Argyll Arms, Soho (p35); Dog & Duck, Soho (p37); the Salisbury, Covent Garden (p16), the Princess Louise, Holborn (p13) and the Tipperary, Holborn (p33), cannot be equalled anywhere: adding on the unique Edwardian (and later) work at the Black Friar, Blackfriars (p28) just adds to the pleasure.

Finally a couple of intriguing localisms. From the Midlands northwards you will regularly see bell-pushes in better rooms. They are now almost entirely non-functioning and were used by customers to summon table service (this still survives in a few Merseyside pubs, by the way). But London – apart from at the Forester, Ealing (p67) – has no historic bell-pushes to the best of our knowledge. We used to think that was because waiter service was not practised but that would be most unlikely and historical sources such as Maurice Gorham (see p148) show this was not the case – so this is something of an enigma.

On the other hand London has one feature we have not met with elsewhere – doors in bar counters. Long-serving licensees tell us they were for servicing the beer engines when these were more complex than they are today. They have been spotted in at least one pub built in the 1950s. Do they really not exist outside London and, if so, why should London be different?

Palm Tree bar doors (p120)

Tunnel (the first underwater thoroughfare in the world) and museum.

History across the road: The Swedish Seamen's Church was opened at 120 Lower Road, Rotherhithe in 1905. The current building dates from 1930 but it was partially rebuilt in 1966-7. See also the Finnish Seamen's Church in Albion Street which was built in 1958 and Rotherhithe Civic Centre and Library which were designed by the same architects as the Finnish Church, Yorke Rosenberg & Mardall. To continue the Scandinavian theme, there is St Olave's, the Norwegian Seamen's Church in Lower Road.

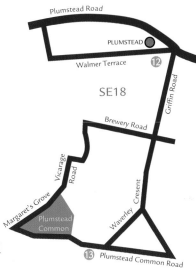

Above: **Albion interior**

LORD DERBY ⑫

89 Walmer Terrace, Plumstead, SE18 7DZ
020 8854 0456
Not listed.
Railway station: Plumstead.

MAP: SE18

This basic, drinkers' pub was built in Victorian times, no doubt with an eye to trade arising from its proximity to Plumstead railway station. It has been extensively opened up but still retains much from a 1930s refitting. The most attractive part is as you enter from the Griffin Road entrance into the former saloon where you are faced with an appealing rounded, panelled bar counter. The saloon also has a skylight in the roof. A wall remains on the right of the entrance but a link has now been cut through it to the space between the counter and the Griffin Road frontage.

The rectangular servery sits in the middle of the pub and would have been the focus for the various surrounding bars. The main feature at the Lord Derby is the extensive, two-thirds-height wall panelling. The name plates on the doors seem original to the 1930s work and include 'club room' which lies on the first floor. It's a pity the counter has now been encumbered by a clumsy gantry.

History round about: Plumstead was a prosperous village with a long history and the church of St Nicholas on High Street has work going back to the 12th century. Suburban development got going with the expansion of Woolwich Arsenal in the early 19th century and the arrival of the railway in 1849.

Below: **Lord Derby interior**

STAR ⑬

158 Plumstead Common Road, SE18 2UL
020 8854 1524
Not listed.
Railway station: Plumstead.

A community local which is something of a puzzle. The pub looks for all the world like an inter-war rebuild yet in the bar furthest down the side road (Jago Close) you will find what appears to be a Victorian bar-back, complete with pretty, flowery mirror strips (note the unusual high-level cupboard in it). The bar counter looks as though it could be of similar vintage, as does the screen that splits the two bars fronting Jago Close.

Anyway this is a very rare survival of a compartmentalised interior in this part of London. The existence of the screen – barely over head height – on the right-hand side is a great rarity and shows how many a street-corner pub would have once been divided up. The part with the mirrored bar-back was evidently once also divided – hence the two entrance doors and the change in counter design. The left-hand side has a single-storey saloon lounge with three-quarter-height panelling, a skylight and a couple of brick fire surrounds. Apart from our Victorian conundrum the fittings are interwar work and include attractive striped glazing in the bar-back and complete tiled schemes in the loos. Note the gas-light fittings – four on the right-hand side and two (with shades) in the saloon lounge.

Above: **Inter-war exterior of the Star**

Below: **Star interior**

CROWN & GREYHOUND ⑭

73 Dulwich Village, Dulwich, SE21 7BJ
020 8299 4976
Grade II listed.
Railway station: North Dulwich.
Real ale.

MAP: SE21 & SE22

A large and much-frequented establishment built as a pub-cum-hotel around 1900 to designs by busy pub architects Eedle & Meyers. The symmetrical exterior is worthy of a good look for such details as the decorative plasterwork, cast-iron lamp standards and light brackets.

<< *LEFT HAND PAGE*

Above: **Seating outisde the Crown & Greyhound**

Below: **Crown and Greyhound interior**

The character has changed greatly inside but on the left-hand side a couple of screens remain from the days when there would have been a multiplicity of rooms. In this area there were bars described as being for 'the lower class of customer' (no such problem today in posh Dulwich). What is now the main bar area was originally known as the saloon and to the right of this, and originally separate from it, was the panelled coffee room. The restaurant used to be a billiard room and at the back left was a skittle alley.

There are some good details of around 1900 remaining in terms of etched glass with the names of some of the former rooms, a good bar-back with plenty of decoration and, over the partition between main bar and former coffee room, some re-sited snob-screens. But don't miss the lavish tall friezes and the impressive ceiling decoration. Also pretty mosaic flooring on the left-hand side from a former corridor. The counters, by contrast, are quite plain.

History in the area: Dulwich Village was once a hamlet and two of its buildings were public houses, the Crown and the Greyhound which were combined into the present pub. In the early 17th century an actor, Edward Alleyn founded Alleyn's College for poor boys. Its full name became 'Alleyn's College of God's Gift at Dulwich' and in 1811-14, after the college had been enriched by a bequest of pictures, Sir John Soane designed the present gallery. Charles Barry jr designed more buildings for the College which were opened on 21 June 1870 and the school took its present name, Dulwich College.

Above: **Wood-panelled interior of the Herne Tavern**

Below: **Herne Tavern exterior**

HERNE TAVERN ⑮

2 Forest Hill Road, Dulwich, SE22 0RR
020 8299 9521
Not listed.
Railway station: North Dulwich, East Dulwich
Real ale.

A beautifully preserved example of inter-war pub-fitting. The original building is Victorian but it was given a thorough remodelling in the 1930s and this work is cherished by the current owners who offer a good balance between drinking and dining.

The window glass tells us that the front left-hand room was the public bar, while the right-hand one was the saloon

lounge. The glass is a lovely survivor with clear, textured panes enlivened by others with mottled green glass. There is a third room behind the public bar: both these left-hand rooms have wall panelling and attractive, original tiled fireplaces. The saloon lounge, extended out from the Victorian pub, has an interesting rounded termination and a very individual red-brick fireplace which is a complete contrast to the others. The bar counters and back fittings are original but quite conventional: the latter, on the saloon lounge side, appears to have had a dumb waiter (currently occupied by wine bottles). Don't miss the quite delightful 1930s chairs in the saloon lounge with their sides made of solid boards and their upward-sweeping arm rests.

You may care to drop in at the Forest Hill Tavern up the road at 118 Forest Hill Road for the remnants of one of Truman's many 1930s schemes. Things to look out for are the superb black glass advertising sign in the right-hand corridor, a lovely inglenook fireplace and the white Vitrolite panelled ceiling.

Above: **Exterior of Blythe Hill Tavern**

Below: **Modest 1920s interior of the Blythe Hill Tavern**

MAP: SE23

BLYTHE HILL TAVERN 🔟

319 Stanstead Road, Forest Hill, SE23 1JB

Not listed.

Railway stations: Catford, Catford Bridge.

Real ale.

A most appealing Victorian corner local, which was given a makeover probably in the 1920s. The exterior tilework of that time has, sadly, been painted over, but doesn't spoil the enjoyment of the interior. There are still three separate rooms with a public bar on the corner, a saloon to the left and a large room running across the back of the pub. There was once a small snug at the back of the public bar entered by the now sealed double doors. The servery has an unusual T-shaped layout designed to create a counter in each of the rooms.

The fittings are typical of their time – plain and undemonstrative in contrast to earlier Victorian exuberance. The counters have plain panelling and the bar-back is also modest but with Tudor arches under the lowest tier of shelves. All the ceilings have exposed beams – not the real thing though: they're just nailed on to create an 'olde worlde' effect. Another sign that the refit was done on a low budget is the use of imitation wood panelling in all the rooms. The fireplaces are pleasing – the one in the rear room with a decorated metal hood and the one in the saloon with a grey-blue tiled surround and a tile with an improbable-looking sailing ship. Attractive benches in the saloon and rear room. An unusual feature is the way customers are free to walk across the serving area between the saloon and rear room.

HALF MOON

10 Half Moon Lane, Herne Hill, SE24 9HU
020 7274 2733
Grade II* listed.
Railway station: Herne Hill.
NI Part Two.
Real ale.

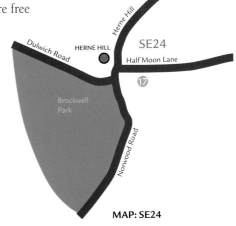

MAP: SE24

A tremendously exuberant piece of pub architecture with some marvellous fittings to match. The architect was J W Brooker and the building went up in 1896. The frivolous style is in some ways reminiscent of the exactly contemporary King's Head in Tooting (p186). As at the King's Head there is a good sense of how the pub was originally divided up into separate rooms. In this case they have been reduced to three. A couple of them are named in the external glazing (which looks like a replacement in the 1930s) which also offers the blandishments of luncheons, snooker and billiards.

The rooms are arranged around an L-shaped servery where the panelled counter and excellent bar-back survive. So does the panelling in the public bar. But the biggest reasons for making a trip here is the 'snug bar', tucked away at the back on the left. This has no fewer than six lovely back-painted mirrors depicting a variety of birds in watery surroundings. Two small labels helpfully inform us that they are the work of 'W Gibbs & Sons glass decorators' of Blackfriars. In this room there is also a screen to the servery – but what a shame the snob screens have been removed from it. Two other screens have etched, cut and coloured glass with pretty lozenges depicting barley, hops and foliage. Four hefty iron columns with Corinthian-style capitals run down the ground floor making sure the upper floors stay where they are.

Above: **Half Moon painted mirror**
Below: **Half Moon interior**

Outer South East

PRINCE FREDERICK ①

31 Nichol Lane, Bromley, BR1 4DE

020 8466 6741

Not listed.

Railway station: Sundridge Park.

Real ale.

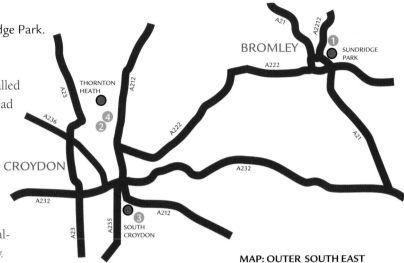

MAP: OUTER SOUTH EAST

There was a pub here called the Prince Frederick's Head in 1761, just ten years after the death of the eponymous prince. The present building is Victorian and, importantly, it was revamped in the 1930s giving it the appealing character it has today.

The two front bars are divided by a wall with a narrow pair of doors allowing access from one side to the other. At one time there must have been an off-sales compartment between the two parts, as suggested by the now disused doorway in the frontage. Both rooms have three-quarter-height wall panelling and distinctive white Vitrolite ceiling panels. In the left-hand room is an attractive dark blue tiled fire surround. The bar counters are plain matchboarded affairs and, as such, difficult to date (they might be later than the 1930s but it's hard to see why they should have been replaced). The bar-back, however, is a distinct 1930s design and has glazed advertising panels.

The rear part is a flat-roofed extension, no doubt, of the 1930s and also has extensive panelling: there seems to have been some opening up in this area.

History in a name: 'Prince Frederick' seems unique as a British pub name and commemorates the eldest son of George II whom he predeceased in 1751. He was a keen cricketer who, the story goes, died after being hit on the head by a cricket ball. Not so – the cause of death was a burst abscess in a lung. Cricket has had its share of fatalities, but our man was not one of them.

Above: **Suburban, inter-war exterior of the Newton Arms**

NEWTON ARMS ②

175 Queens Road, West Croydon, CR0 2PX
020 8684 1654
Not listed.
Railway station: Thornton Heath.

A good example of a three-room inter-war suburban pub for a densely populated area. The frontage is an asymmetrical composition with brown glazed bricks on the ground floor and plenty of half-timbering above. Most of the windows are filled with attractive rippled glass. In the front there are two doors, the right-hand one to the public bar, the left-hand one to the lounge but formerly to an off-sales compartment which, remarkably, still survives even if it is not in use. The original entrance to the lounge was the door halfway down the side.

The servery is L-shaped and extends into both lounge and public bar and (of course) served the off-sales too. The bar counters with their raked tongue-and-grooved panelling are original to the rebuilding of the pub as is most of the woodwork in the bar-backs. At the rear right is a third room which relies on a hatch for access to the servery: its walls have tongue-and-grooved panelling. At the time of our visit the pub was offering an interesting menu of Afro-Caribbean dishes.

SWAN & SUGAR LOAF ③

1 Brighton Road, South Croydon, CR2 6EA
020 8686 2562
Not listed.
Railway station: South Croydon.

Below: **Highly unusual seating in the Swan & Sugar Loaf**

A real landmark hotel-cum-pub of 1896, dramatically designed for a fork in the road and dominated by three great, radiating gables. The architect was Alfred Board of Croydon and his clients the local brewers, Page & Overton who finally ceased production in 1954. Their name is prominently displayed and they were no doubt very pleased with their mighty new pub.

Back in 1896 there would have been numerous internal divisions. These have gone but the counter and rather plain barback are original. But what really makes the visit worthwhile is a rather later addition – the cosy, low snug at the rear dating from perhaps around 1910. It lies behind a wide opening, above which are lovely stained glass representations of two swans and a loaf of sugar. This curious little space has a mighty Jacobean-style fire surround in brown faïence (pity about the out-of-keeping modern copper hood). Either side of this are six highly unusual seats that make the place feel like the drinkers' version of a chapter house in an abbey. On the walls there are a number of historic photographs of the pub.

History in the area: Haling Park is named after Haling Manor which was once owned by Henry VIII. In 1931 Whitgift Grammar School moved to the park from its former premises in the town centre. The school was founded in 1596 by John Whitgift, Archbishop of Canterbury.

VICTORIA CROSS

228 Bensham Lane, Thornton Heath, CR7 7EP
020 8684 3022
Not listed.
Railway station: Thornton Heath.
Real ale

A good example of an inter-war suburban pub, rebuilt in 1937 for an area of dense housing. A crank in the road outside means the pub tapers inwards as it stretches back, making for some unusual spaces. The exterior is a symmetrical composition with buff tile facing below and half-timbering above. Another favourite – rippled glass in the windows – survives in good measure.

There has been some opening up so you can now circumnavigate the central serving area. But, nonetheless, there is still a very good impression to be gained of how the pub was laid out originally. On the left there is the lounge and on the right the public bar, although we were told that originally the functions were reversed. Between the two, at the front, was an off-sales compartment, now merged into the public bar. One of its screens still survives and this has a low access door for staff.

In terms of furnishings, the dominant theme is wooden wall panelling to create the 'olde worlde' feel of 'brewers' Tudor'. The counter and back fittings are largely original but, sadly, rather ungainly superstructures sit on the counter top and mar the appearance of the pub. Access doors in the counter fronts and original tiling in both toilets on the right-hand side.

Above: **Victoria Cross interior**
Below: **Victoria Cross half-timbered exterior**

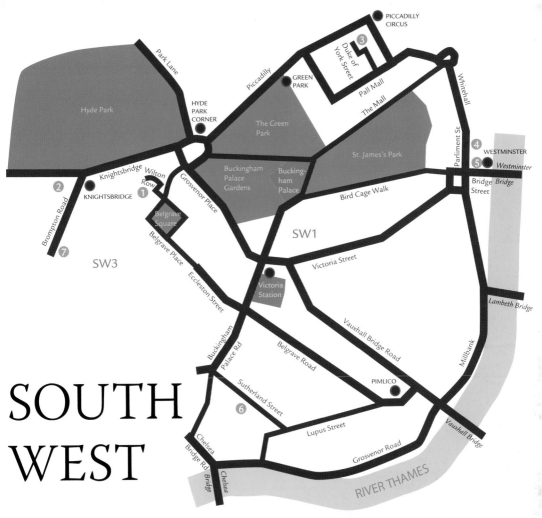

Map labels (clockwise): Park Lane, Piccadilly, PICCADILLY CIRCUS, Duke of York Street, GREEN PARK, Pall Mall, The Mall, Whitehall, HYDE PARK CORNER, Hyde Park, The Green Park, St. James's Park, Parliment St, WESTMINSTER, Westminster, Bridge Bridge, Bridge Street, Bird Cage Walk, Knightsbridge, Wilton Row, Grosvenor Place, Buckingham Palace Gardens, Bucking-ham Palace, SW1, Brompton Road, KNIGHTSBRIDGE, Belgrave Square, Belgrave Place, Eccleston Street, SW3, Victoria Street, Victoria Station, Lambeth Bridge, Buckingham Palace Rd, Belgrave Road, Vauxhall Bridge Road, Millbank, PIMLICO, Sutherland Street, Lupus Street, Grosvenor Road, Vauxhall Bridge, Chelsea Bridge Rd, Chelsea Bridge, RIVER THAMES

SOUTH WEST

SW1 to SW20

GRENADIER ❶

18 Wilton Row, Belgravia, SW1X 7NR
020 7235 3074
Not listed.
Tube: Hyde Park Corner.
Real ale.

Now very much an upmarket place for a drink and a meal, this was once a simple back-street boozer. It was built about 1830 to serve the needs of the staff from the neighbouring mansions and also thirsty guards from a barracks that was located to the west from about 1762 through to 1835. The pub was originally known as the Guardsman. The plain, three-storey Georgian frontage appears much as it did when originally built (apart

MAP: SW1 – SW3

<< *LEFT HAND PAGE*
Paxton's Head glass (p166)

Below: **Grenadier bar pumps**

Above: **Stucco façade of the Grenadier**

Above: **Curved wooden bar in the Paxton's Head**

Below: **Paxton's Head façade**

from the thoroughly unnecessary application of white paint) with stairs up to the main entrance and a door on the side.

The two doors suggest that, small as the pub is, it would have had a couple of separate drinking areas. The fittings are simple and basic as befits what was once an artisan pub – a matchboarded dado round the walls and matchboarded bar counter. The latter has intriguing traces in the centre part that suggest that the panels were removable. At some later stage a pewter top has been placed on the counter.

The two rear rooms have been brought into use in relatively recent years. The left-hand one is dominated by a huge mirror advertising 'Mann, Crossman & Paulin Ltd Old and Mild Ales and Stout' – a reminder of beer styles that in London have now been largely consigned to history.

History in the area: Belgravia was originally called the Five Fields when it was a rural area. In the 1820s it was developed by the Grosvenor family and named Belgrave after one of their country properties. Belgrave Square was mainly designed by Thomas Cubitt in 1826 but some of the terraces and villas were designed by other architects including Sir Robert Smirke. The mews houses here were inhabited by coachmen, grooms and their families. Many famous people have lived in Belgravia and it is also home to many embassies.

PAXTON'S HEAD
153 Knightsbridge, Knightsbridge, SW1X 7PA
020 7589 6627
Grade II listed.
Tube: Knightsbridge.
Real ale.

This popular pub is but a small part of the massive Park Mansions retail and residential redevelopment designed by architect G D Martin: it is located in the phase that was built in 1900-2. There had been a pub on the site for generations and thus we have an interesting example of continuous usage for the licensed trade. The name commemorates Joseph Paxton who designed the Crystal Palace which once stood nearby.

Superlative etched and cut glass can be found lining the walls and in doors and baffles. Motifs include grotesque masks, mythical birds, fruit, flowers and swirling foliage – all stock features in the repertoire of contemporary pub glass designs. Note the doors at the rear right which have PH monograms. The bar counter with its panelled front and the ornate stillion in the middle date back to 1902, as does the central lobby with clock above. There is also an attractive Lincrusta ceiling with foliage decoration. Originally there would have been subdivisions surrounding the counter but these have all been swept away. The superstructure on the counter and bridges to the side walls are modern work.

History in the area: The area of Hyde Park nearest the pub was the site, in 1851, of the Great Exhibition. 230 entries for the building to house it were rejected before Joseph Paxton's stupendous glazed structure, based on the conservatory at Chatsworth House, Derbyshire, where he was garden superintendent, was eventually chosen. It was later moved to Sydenham where it enjoyed a new lease of life until destroyed in a spectacular blaze in 1936.

RED LION

2 Duke of York Street, St James's, SW1Y 6JP
020 7321 0782
Grade II listed.
Tube: Green Park, Piccadilly Circus.
NI Part Two.
Real ale.

Above: **Red Lion exterior**

Below: **Fantastic etched glass inside the Red Lion**

A national treasure! The Red Lion has one of the most spectacular late-Victorian pub interiors anywhere, small but beautifully formed. It is claimed there's been a pub on the site since 1788. The present building went up in 1821 and was given a new pub front in 1871 by architect W H Rawlings though the fittings may date from rather later.

The actual trading area of the pub is tiny and surrounds a central serving area. Yet a century ago, small as it is, it would have been divided up into various separate areas – the three outside doorways are proof of that as are the names 'public bar' and 'private bar' in the door glass. The front part was probably divided up into three while the back area has always been a single space. What makes the Red Lion so special are the superlative etched and cut mirrors lining two of the walls. They create brilliant, glittering reflections to conjure up a magical

Above: **Wood-panelled interior of the Red Lion**

Left: **Red Lion window sign**

Below: **Red Lion exterior decorated with flowers**

atmosphere far removed from the prosaic world of everyday life beyond the pub. The picture is completed by an ornamental ceiling and frieze in both areas. The bar counter at the front has drop-down panels for servicing beer engines in former times – you can see the remains of the keyholes. Don't be fooled by the gantry on the counter top – like nearly all such features they are modern work (see how fresh the woodwork looks).

Near by: If you fancy another pub in the area, try another Red Lion, this one tucked away in Crown Passage off King Street on the west side of St James's Square. It has an interior with old panelling and bar counter, but must have lost a screen that would have created two separate rooms. On the way, look out for the ironwork at Chatham House – at the bottom of Duke of York Street – with surviving snuffers that were used by lamplighters for extinguishing their tapers.

RED LION

48 Parliament Street, Westminster, SW1A 2NH
020 7930 5826
Grade II listed.
Tube: Westminster.
Real ale.

Rebuilt in 1898-9 by architects Gardiner & Theobald in an eclectic Dutch-cum-Renaissance revival style. It's a tall building on a small corner site which suggests the presence of a pub here for a very long time. The ground floor bar has been opened out into a long, single space but originally would have had a couple of drinking areas. The row of columns, glazed screenwork and different levels halfway down the bar suggest a partition at this point. Various good-quality fittings survive and the date of 1900 carved into the bar-back is a helpful record of when they were put in. The bar-back itself has 17th-century-style detail and lots of round arches. The counter has a series of unusually detailed panels with circle motifs.

At the rear of the pub is some excellent etched and polished glass, including a reset panel announcing 'saloon bar'. The ceiling decoration is very pleasing work with square panels and delicate swirling foliage. The rather ungainly structures sitting on the counters are modern pastiche.

THE FUTURE OF OUR HISTORIC PUBS

It is a major aim of this guide to get London's genuine historic pub interiors visited and appreciated. CAMRA also makes a point of drawing them to the attention of planning departments of the London boroughs in which they lie. We believe that with a combination of awareness by the public and pub owners on one hand and local authority vigilance on the other, the pubs listed here should have a bright and long-lived future without damaging change.

Pubs, of course, are commercial businesses and have been constantly changing through time but it does seem sensible both in terms of conserving our heritage and as a matter of good business sense to look after the relatively few genuine old interiors we have left. Surely it is easier to promote a pub with real heritage than yet another one with bland design.

Above: **St Stephen's Tavern exterior**
Below: **'Big Ben' viewed from St
Stephen's Tavern**

History across the road: Sir George Downing MP built Downing Street in the 1680s. Among those who had lodgings there was Dr Johnson's companion, James Boswell. Nowadays only numbers 10, 11 and 12 remain. Number 10 has been the official residence of the Prime Minister since 1732. Interior alterations were designed by Sir John Soane in 1825 and in the late 1950s and early 1960s further alterations were made by Raymond Erith, the architect who designed the famous Hampstead pub, Jack Straw's Castle, now, sadly, converted into residential flats.

ST STEPHEN'S TAVERN
10 Bridge Street, Westminster, SW1A 2JR
020 7925 2286
Grade II listed.
Tube: Westminster.
Real ale.

Opposite the Palace of Westminster and so often busy with tourists, this is a pub to enjoy late-Victorian pub fittings at their grandest. It was built in 1875 and the fittings may well date from that time. Pride of place goes to the extraordinarily tall, eclectically decorated bar-back in the lofty main room. It has five panels of etched and gilded mirrors with swirly foliage, cornucopias and birds in flight: viewed closely the details are a little crude but the overall effect is exotic. High up, over the arched openings is a sequence of mirrored cupboards – it's hard to imagine what they could have been used for. The bar counter is a curvaceous affair with recessed panels. The deeply coffered ceiling is an impressive feature in its own right. In a subsidiary area behind is another Victorian bar-back. There is some original glass in the doors. This pub was well restored by owners Hall & Woodhouse and reopened in 2003 after a long period of closure. Note the new brass lamps: those on the counter are based on glass spirits dispensers which graced some of the most upmarket Victorian pubs. There is a new mezzanine floor.

History across the road: In 1834 a fire destroyed much of the Palace of Westminster including Parliament. The architect Charles Barry's Gothic design for the new buildings was selected out of 97 entries. He was assisted by Augustus Pugin whose designs decorate the interior. The massive tower, housing the famous bell Big Ben is called St Stephen's Tower, hence the name of the pub.

WHITE FERRY HOUSE ⑥

1a Sutherland Street, SW1V 4LD
020 7834 3960
Grade II listed.
Tube: Pimlico.
Real ale.

A locals' pub, which forms a striking landmark in the street-scape and which no doubt doubled as a hotel when built in 1856. The irregular site gives rise to a three-quarter-round corner and a pair of interestingly shaped rooms inside. The public bar lies in the sharp corner and has plain, matchboard panelling to the walls and counter plus a plainish bar-back.

But the real star performer at this pub is the saloon with its late-Victorian panelled bar counter and stunning bar-back. This is a beautiful eight-bay affair with two tiers of paired mirrors with orange-coloured detailing. Sitting on top of it are nine porcelain casks for spirits and other drinks: long disused these are named with their former contents, which included Old Tom (a well-known gin), shrub (lemon or other juice with spirits such as rum), lovage (liquor made from the fruit and seeds of the lovage plant) and aniseed. The windows contain much etched and cut glass. The lamps over the saloon bar counter are evidently imports, bearing the initials of the London, Brighton & South Coast Railway and thus predating 1923.

History round about: The name Pimlico is thought to come from an inn near Victoria Station or a brew served at the inn. The area was largely given over to market gardens but development began in earnest under Thomas Cubitt up to the 1850s.

Above: **Rounded corner of the White Ferry House exterior**

Below: **White Ferry House interior**

BUNCH OF GRAPES ⑦

207 Brompton Road, SW3 1LA
020 7589 4944
Grade II listed.
Tube: Knightsbridge, South Kensington.
Real ale.

This busy pub between Harrod's and the V&A Museum (hence usually crowded with tourists) was put up in 1844: it has three storeys and is now rather dwarfed by neighbouring 20th-century buildings. What is of interest for us here are the fairly substantial vestiges of a late-Victorian refitting. Pride of place goes to a series of back-painted mirrors. The first is in the left-hand lobby and shows grapes hanging off a vine above various flowers. The mirrors continue with five on the left-hand wall showing birds and all sorts of vegetation. They are signed 'W James of Kentish Town' and date from 1890.

It is possible to get a good sense of the way the pub was laid out a century ago. The servery is in the middle and is surrounded by various fragments of screens that would have divided the pub up into a series of separate drinking areas. Particularly notable is the row of five snob screens on the left-hand side with representations of birds and, of course, bunches of grapes. The area where they are located is demarcated by a gross head-height baffle carved with truly gargantuan clusters of grapes. Other historic features are the cast-iron columns supporting the upstairs floors and extensive etched glass.

History nearby: The collections at the Victoria & Albert Museum were formed in 1857 by combining those of the School of Design and the Museum of Ornamental Art (established as the Museum of Manufactures after the Great Exhibition of 1851). The museum complex has developed ever since and today it attracts visitors from all over the world.

The church of St Philip Neri, the Brompton Oratory, was designed in Italian Baroque style by Herbert Gribble who won the commission in 1878 and is the second most important Roman Catholic church in London after Westminster Cathedral.

Above: **Bunch of Grapes etched glass**

ATLAS ⑧

16 Seagrave Road, West Brompton, SW6 1RX
020 7385 9129
Not listed.
Tube and railway station: West Brompton.
Real ale.

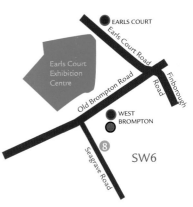

MAP: SW6

A side-street pub which has developed a fine reputation for food and is a classic pub for showing us what major London brewers, Truman's, were up to in the 1930s. The building itself is Victorian but the fittings are a surprisingly complete array from the inter-war refit which provided two distinct rooms, the evidence of which is still apparent today with the public bar (named on the door) at the front.

CLOSED PUBS

The following pubs would all appear in the body of this book but, regrettably, they are closed at the time of writing. We offer brief notes about these historic interiors for the sake of completeness and in the hope that in time you'll find them up and running again.

Barley Mow, Dorset Street, Marylebone, W1U 6QW

Unique for a pair of tiny drinking boxes attached to the bar counter on the left. They are like heightened box-pews in a church. These are about the most extreme example of the how Victorians loved cosy drinking spaces. You would struggle to get more than four or five people into either of them. Grade II listed. National Inventory Part Two.

Crocker's Folly (formerly Crown), Aberdeen Place, Maida Vale, NW8 8JR

A truly magnificent pub-cum-hotel built in 1898. It has superb fittings including a grand entrance with a sumptuous marble fireplace and a white marble counter top. The spacious room on the left was originally a two-table billiard hall. It is also home to London's daftest pub myth. It gets its modern name because its proprietor, Frank Crocker, thought that the Great Central Railway, the last mainline into the capital, would end up near his front door and thus led to no end of business. But it ended up a mile away at Marylebone. Ruin, disaster, despair lead Frank C to jump out of an upper window in his magnificent creation. A tragedy indeed – or it would be if there was a grain of truth in it. Actually the line to Marylebone was given Parliamentary go-ahead in 1893 and trains steamed into the station as the hotel was being completed. In fact Frank died a natural death aged 46 in 1904. He was a much loved and popular landlord and is buried in Kensal Green Cemetery. The tall tale no doubt arises from his early death and amazement at the grandeur of his fine building. Grade II* listed. National Inventory Part Two.

Old Spotted Dog, 212 Upton Lane, Forest Gate, Forest Gate, E7 9EP

A marvellous old building dating back to the 17th century or perhaps earlier. There's a good deal of Victorian or early 20th-century panelling and the vestigial feel of a truly old pub. There is also some pretty traceried woodwork on the walls. The pub was given a vast extension at the rear in 1968. Grade II listed.

Railway Hotel, 38 Station Road, Edgware, HA8 7AD

It is a sad sight to see this large magnificent 'brewers' Tudor' pub looking so forlorn on this busy high street. It was built in 1931 by Truman's in-house architect A E Sewell. Inside most of the fine panelling and half-timbering survive although the room divisions have gone. The adjacent building on the right was originally an off-licence. Grade II listed.

Rayners Hotel, Village Way East, Rayners Lane, HA2 7LX

Huge interwar pub of 1937 by prolific pub architects Eedle & Meyers. Retains much of its original layout and fittings. Grade II listed.

Rose & Crown, 124 Church Street, Croydon, CR0 1RF

A central servery and good fitting in the centre of it with a decorated cornice. There is very pretty stained glass at the front. Not listed.

The room separation is most obvious in the remains of a screen, the glazed top of which survives. Then you will see that the bar counter is treated differently – at the front it is match-boarded and at the back (the plusher end) it has horizontal Art Deco panelling with a rounded corner. The bar-backs, however, are similar and there is also a black-and-white tiled spittoon. Also from the 1930s are the fixed seating and three brick fire surrounds each with a small terracotta relief – a galleon, a hunting scene and a frisky stag. There is wall panelling in the rear area with advertisements for Truman's wares and a promotional mirror over one of the fireplaces. The counter fronts have doors, a feature of many a London pub in times past, to allow servicing of the beer engines.

History nearby: Brompton Cemetery, consecrated in 1840, is one of the greatest Victorian London cemeteries and contains many fine monuments. Buried here are Emmeline Pankhurst (1928), Francis Fowke (1865), architect of the Albert Hall, and Henry Cole (1882) who organised the Great Exhibition and the Victoria and Albert Museum.

Above: **Atlas exterior**

Below: **Matchboarded bar in the Atlas**

DUKE OF EDINBURGH ⑨

204 Ferndale Road, Brixton, SW9 8AG
020 7924 0509
Not listed.
Tube and railway station: Brixton.
Real ale.

MAP: SW9

Below: **Duke of Edinburgh glass**

A beautifully crafted piece of 1930s suburban pub architecture by Truman's, it has three storeys and is faced with attractive thin red bricks which have also been used for the window linings and mullions.

Inside you can now perambulate through the whole pub but can still get a good sense of the way it was originally arranged. The public bar was at the front and more simply appointed than the more upmarket rear areas, e.g. a matchboard counter in contrast to the panelled ones behind – note all the counters have doors for servicing the original beer engines as was usual in Truman's 1930s pubs. The light-coloured oak woodwork is typical of the colouration and quality of what they put into their pubs, as is the distinctive advertising lettering in the bar-backs, the chequerwork spittoon trough in the rear area,

the use of mirrors over the fireplaces and the (now disappeared) sliding screen that would have split the rear parts. The inglenook with Tudor-arched fireplace and adjacent seating is particularly attractive.

A notable feature is the extensive rear garden approached down a passage at the rear and which shows how inter-war pub builders had in mind the need to encourage not just hardened drinkers but couples and families who might enjoy sitting out in good weather.

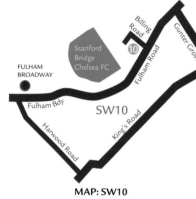

MAP: SW10

Above: **Fox & Pheasant inter-war chairs and tables**

Below: **Fox & Pheasant exterior**

FOX & PHEASANT ⑩

1 Billing Road, West Brompton, SW10 9UJ
020 7352 2943
Not listed.
Tube: Fulham Broadway.
NI Part One.
Real ale.

A real inter-war time-warp now owned by East Anglian brewers Greene King and set in a private, gated-off road close to the Chelsea football ground. It was built in 1896 as the Prince of Wales, changed its name to Bedford Arms about ten years later and then to Fox and Pheasant in 1965. It was licensed simply as a beer house until as late as 1953.

As you enter there is a small lobby with an off-sales hatch to the servery and doors to the public bar (left) and the rather larger saloon bar (right). Everything is quite low-key and what we see is typical of run-of-the-mill pub-fitting between the wars. The servery has glazed areas on each side, which house the spirits and glasses, etc. The rear doors and windows have attractive dimpled glass with green bands. All the fittings are from the inter-war refit as are some quite delightful tables and chairs with raked or curved legs. It's a real pity the tiled frontage has been painted over.

History nearby: Note St Mark's College chapel on the south side of Fulham Road designed by the architect Edward Blore in 1881 in Romanesque style.

FALCON ⑪

2 St John's Hill, Battersea, SW11 1RU
020 7924 8041.
Grade II listed.
Railway station: Clapham Junction.
NI Part Two.
Real ale.

MAP: SW11

On a corner, this busy pub is right in the heart of Battersea's shopping area and was built in 1887 when it doubled up as a hotel for travellers (handy for Clapham Junction station) and a pub for locals. It's a showy piece of architecture, typical of the time that it was built.

What really counts is the interior. In the middle is a large serving area enclosed by a curvaceous counter which is claimed as the longest in Britain (its only real rival is the Horseshoe Bar in Drury Street, Glasgow). In the centre of the servery is a very tall back fitting, an office and stairs to the cellar. A great deal of the original arrangements survive and give an idea of what a big, quite classy, London pub looked like a century ago. In the angle of the roads is a large public bar (originally with internal partitions) and at the rear is a luxuriously panelled room with wood carvings and a large timber fire surround (pity about the garish modern glass in the pair of skylights). On the left-hand side is a snug, enclosed by a glass and timber screen. Adjacent to this is a lobby entrance where original glasswork has portrayals of the eponymous falcon and the words 'private bar'. The most notable glass, however, is in the rear room where there are painted depictions of the pub in its humble pre-1887 guise and its present, grander manifestation. One of these shows funeral carriages stopping off at 'Death's Door', the nickname for the pub when its landlord happened to be a Mr Death.

History next door: Clapham Junction Station opened in 1863 and became one of the busiest railway junctions in the world (still the busiest in Britain). The area around the station is now a busy shopping district dominated by the imposing Debenham's department store (formerly Arding and Hobbs) built in 1910 to a design by James Gibson.

Above: **The longest bar in Britain at the Falcon**

Below: **Falcon exterior**

PAVILION ⑫

135 Battersea Park Road, Battersea, SW11 4LR
020 7622 4001
Not listed.
Railway stations: Battersea Park, Queenstown Road.
Real ale.

This community local is a plain 1930s rebuild and one that retains a good deal of its original fittings. The best room is at the rear, entered from Havelock Terrace, which is roughly square in plan and keeps its two-thirds-height panelling, panelled bar counter and bar-back. Even the beige, grey-blue and black tiling at the base of the counter is original and looks quintessentially 1930s. The front bar also has its original counter but the bar-back seems to be a replacement.

Other things to note are the very complete set of window glass – large frosted panels surrounded by dimpled work – and the 1930s tiling in the loos. The ladies' off the rear room still has its venerable porcelain 'Amor Automatic' cistern!

A few yards away in the same block at 21 Bradmead is Flanagan's, another inter-war pub. It is now a one-room bar but retains its counter, panelling and some nice wooden fire surrounds and is well worth a visit.

History over the road: Across the busy Battersea Park Road is the Battersea Dogs and Cats Home, the oldest and most famous of its kind in the country. It began life in Holloway in 1860 amid Victorian concern about animal welfare and moved here in 1871.

Above: **Understated exterior of the Pavilion**

Below: **Wood-panelled 1930s bar in the Pavilion**

Below: **Beamed interior of the Windsor Castle**

WINDSOR CASTLE ⑬

36 St John's Hill, Battersea, SW11 1SA
020 7228 1708.
Not listed.
Railway station: Clapham Junction.
Real ale.

This drinkers' pub may have disappeared by the time you wish to visit as it is threatened with demolition to make way for redevelopment. But, as we write, it is just up the hill from the main entrance to Clapham Junction railway station. It is a classic example of a 'brewers' Tudor' pub which still conveys much of its original layout and feel. Across the front of the pub is a smallish public bar with typical inter-war wall panelling. But what really matters is the back room which is probably the result of an amalgamation of two. The rear part is a first-rate example of one of a 'brewers' Tudor' attempt at creating a medieval-style hall. This one has panelled walls and hefty, rustically treated timbers to the roof trusses – no doubt concealing very 'un-Tudor' steel beams. Note how much use is made of imitation adzed tooling on the timbers to enhance ye olde effect. There are also dormer windows and an attractive brick fire surround. The bar counters seem original work but there has been much renewal in the back fittings.

History in the area: Battersea was famous for its market gardens and especially for its asparagus which was sold in 'Battersea bundles'. From the late 17th century several industries flourished including copper works, lime works and milling.

Above: **Timbered exterior of the Windsor Castle**

DUKE OF DEVONSHIRE ⑭

39 Balham High Road, Balham, SW12 9AN
020 8673 1363
Not listed.
Tube: Balham, Clapham South.
Railway station: Balham.
Real ale

This is a substantial brick, corner-site pub, probably refitted in the late 1890s when, no doubt, the pink granite facing was fitted on the ground floor.

There has been a great deal of opening out and replacement of fittings internally but this pub is included here for the startling and impressive amount of high quality glass. Most notable is the row of etched and coloured mirrors lining the blind wall of the front bar, and also the etched mirror glass in the bar-back in the rear saloon. There are doors with etched and coloured glass bearing the name 'saloon'. In complete contrast is the inter-war glass in the front bar outside windows where pretty, coloured pieces are interspersed randomly in the rippled and plain panes. The bar counter in the front bar is probably late-Victorian. You should also note the grid design of the ceilings throughout.

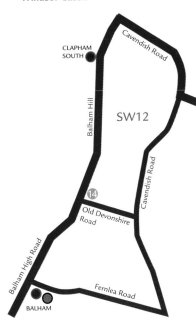

MAP: SW12

Below: **Duke of Devonshire exterior**

History at the front door: Balham High Road follows the route of the Roman road, Stane Street which ran from Chichester to London. The coming of the underground to Balham must have been a great boon. In 1926 a poster advertising the opening of Balham underground station dubbed it the 'gateway to the south' a phrase later famously used in a sketch by the comedian Peter Sellers, albeit in a more ironic manner.

HARE & HOUNDS

216 Upper Richmond Rd, East Sheen, SW14 8AH
020 8876 4304
Not listed.
Grade II listed.
Railway station: Mortlake.
Real ale.

A plain, buff brick, three-storeyed Georgian inn standing proudly on the road leading from London out to Richmond and the oldest building in an area full of inter-war housing. It has been substantially modified over the years and this includes a thorough re-working of the interior in the 1930s. The parts on the right-hand side have been transformed by opening up in the last few decades but there is still a good deal of quality work left from the 1930s.

The reason for inclusion here is the rather remarkable survival of the small public bar on the left-hand side. It is entered either by a side door from the wagon entrance on the left or through a screen immediately on the left of the main front entrance. The oak fittings are typical of the restrained work of the 1930s, such as the elegantly boarded counter and simply detailed, rectilinear bar-back (the designs recur in the right-hand room). This public bar still has the feel of a community pub where (mostly) elderly locals come to meet. The lounge bar and the extensive garden are more what one would expect in affluent Sheen.

History in the area: Mortlake, between Sheen and the Thames, was famous for its tapestry works in the 17th century but this closed in 1703 after the quality of the raw materials declined. Another industry that flourished was brewing and this continues at the Stag Brewery in Mortlake High Street although, sadly, it no longer produces real ale but that dismal attempt at beer, Budweiser.

<< *LEFT HAND PAGE*
Duke of Devonshire glass detail

MAP: SW14

Above: **Hare & Hounds interior**
Below: **Georgian portico outside the Hare & Hounds**

PROTECTING OUR HISTORIC PUBS

A fair proportion of all the public houses in this book are officially 'listed' as buildings of architectural or historic importance and this gives them some protection from damaging change. There are three grades of listing: II, II* and I. Grade IIs make up 94% of all listings and this is the grade of most of the listed pubs in this book. A few make it to II* which puts them in an elite 4% while the George in Southwark has a Grade I listing for being one of the country's last galleried coaching inns.

Contrary to popular belief, listing is not about preventing change. Rather, the purpose is to manage it responsibly. If any significant changes are planned, listed building con-sent must be sought from the local planning authority and, in the case of Grade II* and Grade I buildings, English Heritage will normally have a strong input.

For pubs in this book which are not listed this does not mean they lack any historic value. It is simply that they do not meet the very stringent national criteria of architectural or historic merit. They still have features of historic value and also provide a vital link for local communities with their past. These communities are often vociferous (and often successful) in protecting their pubs against unnecessary and expensive change dreamed up by pub-owners intent on making their estates conform to some stereotyped formula or 'brand'.

We believe all the pubs in this guide are worthy of protection and sensitive treatment. Where statutory listing is lacking, we urge local planning authorities to add the pubs to their 'local list' of historic buildings. These are an important way of enabling local authorities and communities to appreciate the building stock in their care. Although they have no legal force at the present time, local lists have often been a means of shaping local plans and encouraging the developers to look after pubs more sympathetically, thus saving them expense and preserving an asset for the community.

King's Head's magnificent Grade II listed exterior

DUKE'S HEAD ⑯

8 Lower Richmond Road, Putney, SW15 1JN
020 8788 2552
Grade II listed.
Railway station: Putney.
Real ale.

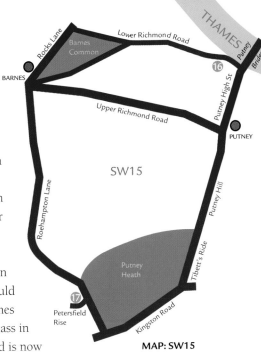

A touch of Victorian pub splendour where you can enjoy a drink and a meal overlooking the Thames. It was built in 1864 and then altered in 1894 which is no doubt the date of the impressive set of interior fittings.

The pub comes in three distinct areas, now all interlinked but a century ago there would have been no such free-flowing spaces. Each outside door would have led to its own separate drinking area. The names 'public bar' and 'saloon lounge' survive in etched glass in two of the doors. The rear room has no counter and is now primarily a dining area with impressive views over the river. A full-height screen, with large panes of etched glass, mark it off from the rest of the pub.

The front parts of the Duke's Head have an island servery. Its central stillion has a modern base but Victorian upper parts with pretty coving ornamented by floral swags. A screen slices through the back part of the servery and is filled with etched and cut glass with flowers and swirling decoration which are to be found in other glasswork here. The bar counter is divided into broad panels, each of which has the characteristic London feature of opening (in this case drop-down) doors. You should also note the glass advertising the entrance to the club room which is located upstairs.

The most recent alterations to the pub were in 2006 which opened up the circulation and involved, sadly, cutting an unnecessarily wide opening in the screen located nearest the corner of the pub.

History through the window: The stretch of the Thames running through Putney is most famous as the start of the annual Oxford and Cambridge Boat Race. The first of these was rowed in 1829 and it then became an annual event (apart from during the two world wars) from 1856. As at 2007 Cambridge lead 79-73 (with one dead heat since 1829). The Head of the River race is also rowed every year on the same course.

Above: **Inside the Duke's Head**
Below: **Duke's Head at night**

Above: **Highwayman interior**

Above: **Gorringe Park exterior**
Below: **Fielded panelling inside the Gorringe Park**

HIGHWAYMAN ⑰

13 Petersfield Rise, Roehampton, SW15 4AE
020 8780 1686
Not listed.
Real ale

This 1950s estate pub is a rare example of its time. It sits on a sharp hill among the tower blocks of the London County Council's Alton East estate which was mainly built in 1952-5. It is typical of the simple, angular architecture typical of its day. External ornamentation is confined to a couple of vertical strips with pierced circles and the compressed hexagonal motifs on the walls and in the doors. The pub was built with a public bar (right) and saloon (left) either side of a central, disused off-sales and doorway to private accommodation. Apparently a 'family room' was added on the left in the 1980s.

The two original rooms are simply appointed, the saloon having some wall panelling with imitation marquetry strips, a brick fireplace and contemporary clock above. It was, at some point, expanded into the open porch area shown in the historic photograph. The public bar room is disused, a sign of changing social habits in Roehampton that have led to several pub closures. The counters are original but the saloon bar-back was altered in around 2004.

History in a name: The pub name comes from highwayman Jerry Abershaw who plied his trade in the area and was hanged for it in 1795. The story goes that his last wish was to be hanged without his shoes to disprove his mother's optimistic prediction that he would die with his boots on.

GORRINGE PARK ⑱

29 London Road, Tooting, SW17 9HW
020 8648 4478
Not listed.
Railway station: Tooting.
Real ale.

Right by Tooting railway station, this Young's corner pub has work from two main periods. The building itself, a three-storey piece of Italianate-style architecture, probably dates from about 1875 but it was given a makeover during the inter-war years, hence the brown and buff tile facing to the ground floor (recently and disgracefully painted over).

There are still two rooms, the better of which is the 'saloon lounge' (as it calls itself) at the rear which has two-thirds-height fielded panelling, no doubt dating from the inter-war remodelling. The fireplace with small red bricks and the mirror over it, and textured window glass are part of the same scheme, as are the panelled bar counter and the bar-back. A winding corridor leads round to the public bar at the front. Judging by the three extant and former doorways this would no doubt have been subdivided a century ago. The basic matchboard panelling in this room points up the differing furnishing schemes between the front and the back. There is an old cast-iron fireplace in the public bar but the counter there looks like a relatively modern replacement. Sadly the counters of both rooms are disfigured by clumpy, modern pot-shelves.

The name of the pub is said to have come from an estate that lay in the area before the oceans of bricks and mortar arrived.

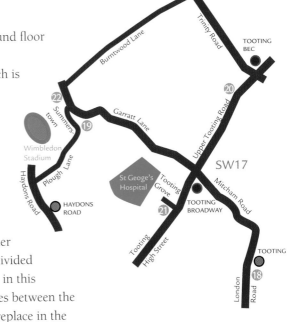

MAP: SW17

HARE & HOUNDS ⑲
(formerly White Lion)
99 Summerstown, Tooting, SW17 0BQ
020 8946 6030.
Not listed.
Railway station: Haydons Road.

Below: **Hare & Hounds wood-panelled interior**

A corner-site pub which seems to have been remodelled either just before or just after World War I. The exterior has some very attractive stained glass window details of stylised flowers, leaves and hearts. The interior retains its three-room character and its central serving area. There is a screen dividing two of the rooms from one another, while a wall between the corner bar and the room on Summerstown has simply had a small opening pierced in it. The woodwork is restrained with fielded panelling on the walls and a plain panelled bar counter. The depressed arches in the bar-back are very typical of their time. There is an attractive entrance lobby on the angle of the streets. The name of the pub was changed in autumn 2007.

Above: **Etched glass inisde the King's Head**

Below: **Toby plaques outside the Little House**

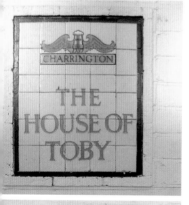

KING'S HEAD ⑳

84 Upper Tooting Road, Tooting, SW17 7PB
020 8767 6708
Grade II listed.
Tube: Tooting Bec.
NI Part Two.
Real ale.

This is one of the most exotic confections among London's pubs and was built in 1896 by the prolific pub architect, W M Brutton. Inside one can still get a good sense of how a lavish late-Victorian pub was organised and fitted up.

Down both sides are tiled corridors that led into various drinking areas – you have to visualise every external or corridor door leading into a separate room or compartment. These were all served across a large, central counter with rounded ends. In the middle of this servery is a delightful island bar-back with delicate detail and an especially attractive octagonal display feature. Also note the etched glass in the outside windows and internal screens, the timber and plaster arches straddling the servery, the filigree of its supporting brackets, and the lovely friezes of various patterns and sizes.

The original spaces would have been relatively small for the most part, especially on the right-hand side. However, at the back is a large, long room with skylights that would probably have served as a billiard room, a feature that was common in many large late-Victorian pubs. The screen between it and the rest of the pub is magnificent with etched panels decorated with swags of foliage, ribbons, etc. Note the difference in quality between the original etched glass and the modern replacements.

LITTLE HOUSE (formerly Queen Victoria) ㉑

13 Tooting Grove, Tooting, SW17 0RA
020 8672 3265
Not listed.
Tube: Tooting Broadway.
Real ale.

Originally called the Queen Victoria, this pub was built in 1934 as part of the surrounding housing estate. It is quite plain externally and has a green-tiled roof that is so typical of its time, as are the metal windows (set within timber frames). What a shame someone decided to paint the brickwork cream!

Inside there are two separate rooms, each with half-length panelling and brick fire surrounds (the one on the left is particularly appealing with its wavy tiles set in the lintel). The counters and back fittings are original too and in both counters you can see examples of doors which were used as access to service the beer engines behind.

Between the two rooms there was once an off-sales compartment (hence the now disused external door). One of its lateral screens survives, complete with a low doorway to enable staff to get round the pub without going outside. The screen also has, most curiously, a false, full-height pair of doors, apparently just for show.

PRINCE OF WALES

646 Garratt Lane, Tooting, SW17 0NT
020 8946 2628
Not listed.
Railway stations: Earlsfield, Haydons Road.
Real ale.

This Young's pub is one of so many rebuilt during the great London pub boom – in this case in 1898 – and its original, Victorian appearance can be seen in an old photograph displayed in the left-hand part of the building (which originally formed a billiard room).

But between the wars there was an extensive remodelling so now we have here an interesting combination of Victorian and c.1930 work. The latter is most conspicuously represented by the buff external tiling which was very popular at the time to give pubs a sleek, up-to-date appearance, far removed from the ornate Victorian character displayed in the photograph mentioned above. However, some aspects of the original building were not so easy (or sensible) to efface, hence we have the old Lincrusta ceiling, cast-iron columns, bar counter and central fitting, tiled floor at the Garratt Lane entrance and the screen which splits the pub into two main bars. The inter-war work involves the glazing, brick fireplaces and entrance doors in the Summerstown entrance lobby. There is good Victorian etched and cut glass in the former billiard room.

Above: **Prince of Wales entrance tiles**
Below: **Prince of Wales exterior**

Top: **Alma interior plaques**

Above: **Alma exterior**

Left: **Original wood staircase, with etched mirrors, inside the Alma**

ALMA

499 Old York Road, Wandsworth, SW18 1TF

020 8870 2537

Not listed.

Railway station: Wandsworth Town.

Real ale.

The Alma, now a smart dining pub owned by Young's, has the vestiges of a truly sumptuous decorative scheme from around 1900. The pub is right opposite Wandsworth Town Station from which the name can be seen writ large in the parapet: it commemorates the Crimean War battle of 1854 and was no doubt built shortly afterwards. The ground floor has vivid green tiling of about 1900.

Inside, the large servery sits in the middle of a now wholly opened-up area. The outstanding feature is a series of back-painted mirrors with flowers, foliage and birds (mainly herons considering their next meal): the mirrors even line the stairs to the upstairs function room. In an alcove there is a lovely fireplace with another painted mirror above (note also the original gas-light fittings).

The other notable decorative feature is a series of three mosaic roundels surrounded by flecked grey marble frames and bearing the name of the pub. The woodwork is high-quality work: note the bar counter furthest from the main road – it's on a truly gigantic scale. Some etched glass also survives in the lobby on the corner and to the former billiard room at the rear (now a restaurant). Here there is a deep classical frieze of swirly foliage and naked youths.

JACK BEARD'S IN THE FOG
(formerly Country House) 24

2 Groton Road, Earlsfield, SW18 4EP

020 8874 2715

Not listed.

Railway station: Earlsfield.

Real ale.

This street-corner local, now named as a member of the Jack Beard's chain, was built near Earlsfield station in Victorian times as the Country House. 'The Fog' was a nickname (from the days

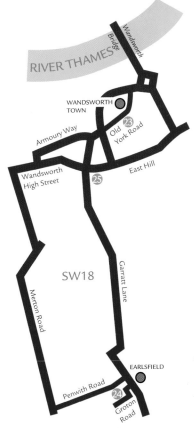

MAP: SW18

Above: **Jack Beard's in the Fog, brass door signage**

Below: **Jack Beard's in the Fog interior**

THE CAMRA NATIONAL INVENTORY

The *National Inventory of Pub Interiors of Outstanding Historic Importance* (*National Inventory* for short) is CAMRA's pioneering initiative to identify and publicise the most historic pub interiors left throughout the UK. The list as at 2007 is published in the *Good Beer Guide 2008* while fuller descriptions plus photographs are available at **www.heritagepubs.org.uk**. The *National Inventory* comes in two parts: Part One consists of historic interiors which are listed for their intactness while Part Two contains ones which, although altered, still retain features or rooms of truly national significance.

when London had fogs/smogs) bestowed by those who tarried here on the way home to their nearest and dearest and attributed their tardy return to being delayed by the fog.

The pub was given a total refit about 1930 and still retains its three separate rooms, each of which bears striking brass plates with the name in question – public bar (on the corner), private bar, and – perhaps unique – meal room. The fittings are plain but elegant with half-height wall panelling, simple bar counter and black and white tiling in front of it. There are exposed beams, typical of c.1930, to the ceilings. There is a dumb waiter in the private bar, sliding doors from the meal room to the public bar, and a hatch to the servery. Note also the three surviving gaslight fittings.

SPREAD EAGLE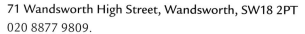

71 Wandsworth High Street, Wandsworth, SW18 2PT
020 8877 9809.
Grade II listed.
Railway station: Wandsworth Town.
Real ale.

A lavish late-Victorian Young's pub rebuilt in 1898 as part of the great pub boom. It's a landmark Renaissance-style building facing the former, much lamented Young's Brewery. The interior gives a very good idea of what a classy pub was meant to look like a hundred years ago. There are three rooms separated by screens though it is evident that the left-hand part was formerly subdivided (see the multiple doors and entrance mosaic to the 'public bar'). The big room on the right is huge and probably always was a single space. It has a staircase leading to the upstairs rooms. Then comes a screen to the 'dining room and lounge' at the rear left. This area is largely newly fitted.

All areas at the Spread Eagle are connected by a three-sided servery, still with its original counter and back fittings (note the unusual pierced work in the spandrels) and most impressive these are too: like the screens they have great expanses of etched glass which makes the whole pub sparkle. The distinctive and attractive canopy over the main entrance is modern.

History across the road: Young's Ram Brewery complex is one of the finest in the UK and retains buildings and machinery of considerable importance. It is Grade II* listed but includes three

Top left: **Fox & Grapes interior**

Top right: **Fox & Grapes stained glass**

Left: **Fox & Grapes sign**

Grade II-listed buildings: the 18th-century former Brewer's House, 19th-century stables and Brewery Tap pub. The latter was built in 1883 as part of a rebuilding scheme by Henry Stock who was later the company architect for Charrington's brewery. It was remodelled in the 1930s and was known as the Ram Inn until 1974. Sadly, brewing ceased in September 2006 and was transferred to the Charles Wells site in Bedford. The site has now been sold for redevelopment.

FOX & GRAPES

Camp Road, Wimbledon, SW19 4UN
020 8946 5599
Not listed.
Railway Station: Wimbledon
Tube: Wimbledon
Real ale.

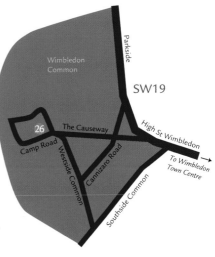

MAP: SW19

The destination pub is nothing new. The Fox & Grapes seems to have been developed to attract visitors to Wimbledon Common in the early 20th century (as it still does).

The story starts with the two-storeyed left-hand part which is probably Victorian. It is a low room with full-height matchboard wall and also ceiling panelling, and gives a good idea how many a small, plain, outer suburban pub in London must have looked before the use of mass transport and consumerism. The bar counter is a modern addition, however.

The left-hand room was the public bar and is a contrast to the 'saloon lounge' on the right. This part is said to have been developed on the site of the former stabling and is probably a remodelling in the inter-war period to cater for visitors to the Common. It is a deliberate attempt at an 'olde worlde' feel with exposed roof trusses and beams. The window glass is dimpled and has pretty splashes of little green hearts and other decoration. The counter, panelling and fireplace are all well crafted work. The illuminated lettering with the name of the pub probably dates from the 1960s.

History nearby: Eagle House in Wimbledon High Street was built in 1613 for Robert Bell, one of the founders of the East India Company. In 1887 it was owned and restored by the architect T G Jackson. In the early 19th century it became a school and a stone eagle was placed on the central gable, hence the name. It was later converted to offices.

Above: **Manor interior**

Left: **Crest of Hodgsons' Kingston Brewery on the Duke of Buckingham façade**

Outer South West

DUKE OF BUCKINGHAM

104 Villiers Road, Kingston-
upon-Thames, KT1 3BB
0020 8546 8533
Not listed.
Railway station: Berrylands.

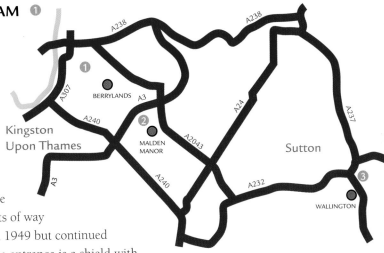

MAP : OUTER SOUTH WEST

A suburban, red-brick
pub built in the 1930s by
Hodgsons' Kingston Brewery
– named on a cast-iron plaque
low down outside about rights of way
(Hodgsons ceased brewing in 1949 but continued
bottling until 1965). Over the entrance is a shield with
the three salmon from the borough arms and a rebus with
K and a tun (see picture, left). These features and the general
architectural style reappear at the Hodgsons' contemporary,
but larger, Manor pub in Malden Manor. As you enter you can't
miss the attractive and most unusual curved doors – left to the
public bar and, right, to a large room, which is now an amalgamation of two original ones. The outside door to the rear
portion has now been blocked off. Perhaps the most notable
feature is the octagonal, leaded skylight over the servery. There
is also some original work in the fireplace, panelling, counters,
parts of the stillion in the centre of the servery and curved
cornices to the ceilings. The area beyond the arch in the rear
room was once a kitchen.

Above: **Duke of Buckingham interior**
Below: **Duke of Buckingham red-
brick exterior**

MANOR ❷

Manor Drive North, Malden Manor, KT3 5PN
020 8335 3199
Not listed.
Railway station: Malden Manor.
Real ale.

Often offering interesting real ales the Manor is prominently
sited on a roundabout in an inter-war housing estate and hand-
ily placed by Malden Manor station. The pub is believed to have
opened in 1938, is built of red brick and has similarities to the

Above: **Manor exterior**

rather smaller Duke of Buckingham in Kingston. Both were built by Hodgsons' Kingston Brewery which was founded way back around 1610.

This is a big pub which remarkably, and very rarely, in these parts, still has three separate rooms. The public bar (right) and private bar (on the corner) are little altered but the huge space on the left is an amalgamation of the 'saloon' and 'luncheon room' (so-named in the glass of the door at the back facing the station). The panelled bar counter and canopy over are original (but not the columns in between). The bar-back is also largely original and there is petty Art Deco-style decoration to the cornices and striking interlocked circles over the external doors.

DUKE'S HEAD HOTEL ❸

6 Manor Road, Wallington, SM6 0AA
020 8401 7410
Grade II listed.
Railway station: Wallington.
Real ale.

Above: **Duke's Head Hotel interior**

Below: **Outside the Duke's Head Hotel on a sunny day**

This busy Young's house is in a mid-19th-century, white stuccoed building in the old village centre of Wallington. It overlooks an attractive green which is much used by pub customers in decent weather. The pub has expanded mightily in recent times, not least due to the grafting on of a hotel on the right-hand side.

However, it does still have separate rooms and, if you mentally block out the large dining room at the rear, quite a lot of the atmosphere from a refitting in the 1930s. At that time there were four pub rooms, all of which are still clearly traceable. The most complete is the public bar, a plainly furnished room on the corner which has an original curved bar counter. The main area consists of three interlinked spaces. The front one, with the main entrance, has a delightful little snug leading off it, complete with panelling, marble fire surround and a 1930s counter. Right off the entrance is a large panelled area where the most unusual feature is a 1930s clock with screwed-on numbers. Behind, the rear area is dark and dominated by heavy timbers which are tooled to create the 'olde worlde' look that was so popular among pub-builders and pubgoers between the wars: it also has a brick fire surround with a Tudor arch.

Glossary

Ale: originally a fermented malt liquor, made without the use of hops. The term has been effectively interchangeable with 'beer' for at least the last 200 years – as in the term 'real ale'.

Arts and Crafts: a late 19th-century English artistic and architectural movement that emphasised the value of handicraft and good design as against mass-production methods.

Art Deco: a fashionable style between the wars. It relies on sleek lines and geometrical patterns. The name comes from the Exposition Internationale des Arts-Decoratifs held in Paris in 1924-5, which greatly enhanced its popularity.

Art Nouveau: a style relying on flowing lines and sinuous forms often based on nature and the human fugure. It was popular between about 1890 and 1914 but more in Europe than the UK. It was, however, quite popular for aspects of pub decoration.

Bar-back: shelving, sometimes very ornately treated and incorporating mirors, at the rear of a servery.

Barrel: a 36-gallon (164-litre) cask and once the most popular vessel for beer. Casks of other capacities have other names: the nine-gallon (41-litre) containers so widely used today are known as firkins.

Beer: fermented malt liquor made using hops. Hops, used in Britain since the 14th century, impart flavour and aid the keeping properties of the beer. The term has been effectively interchangeable with 'ale' for at least the last 200 years – as in the term 'real ale'. The term embraces lager.

Beer engine: a device for raising beer from the cellar, nearly always referring to a hand-pump.

Bitter: a light, highly hopped beer which appeared in the late 19th century and became increasingly popular in the 20th.

Brewers' Tudor: an architectual style popular in the early 20th century which drew nostalgically upon the half-timbered architecture of the Tudor period.

Cask: a barrel-shaped container for beer: can be of various sizes, each of which has its own name. The term 'barrel', strictly-speaking, holds 36 gallons (164 litres).

Faïence: blocks or slabs of earthenware, glazed after an initial firing. The name comes from Faenza, a major Italian centre for glazed pottery in Italy.

Gin palace: an early 19th-cenrty term for a lavishly appointed establishment concentrating on spirits consumption (especially gin). It is also used in relation to ornate late-Victorian pubs: this usage, strictly speaking, is inaccurate but no other terms has arisen to encapsulate them.

Hand-pump: the lever on the bar counter which operates a beer engine (q.v.) draws beer from the cask in the cellar and now standard method of dispensing real ale.

Jug and bottle: a small section of a pub, usually with its own entrance off the street, where drink could be purchased for consumption off the premises.

Lager: lager differs in a number of respects from traditional British beers. It relies on bottom (rather than top) fermentation and that fermentation takes place at a lower temperature, including a secondary fermentation for a long period at around 0° C (32° F) (The word 'larger' comes from the German word for a store). Different malts and hops are also used.

Loggia: an arcaded space, roofed, but open on at least one side, typically overlooking a garden.

Lounge: a better-class pub room.

Mild: a low-gravity beer, normally dark in colour. Popular, especially as working man's drink (see pp.74-5), it all but vanished between the 1960s and 1980s.

Off-sales: sales of drink for consumption off the licensed premises. The term is sometimes applied to the place in the pub where the sales takes place and which also goes by various other names such as jug and bottle.

Porter: a dark, strong, bitter-tasting beer popular in London and the South-East since the 1720s (see pp.74-5).

Pot-shelf: a shelf over a bar counter for housing glasses. They appear to be a late 20th-century development and have profoundly affected the appearance and atmospere of many pubs.

Private bar: a more select and smaller area than the public bar. The name implies occupancy by a group of regulars known to one another.

PubCo: a pub-owning company with no brewing interests. They arose following the Beer Orders of 1989 (see p.142) which limited the number of pubs a brewery could own.

Real ale: a term coined in the early 1970s to describe traditional beer which undergoes a secondary fermentation and conditioning in the cask (hence the use of the term 'cask-conditioned').

Saloon: a better-class pub room.

Servery: the area, almost always behind a bar counter, from which drinks are dispensed.

Snob screen: a range of small, swivelling, translucent glazed panels at eye level that provided customers a degree of privacy.

Snug: a small, intimate drinking space.

Spittoon (trough): a receptacle or trough for spit and accumulating cigarette and cigar ends and other sundry detritus.

Stillion: a fitting in the middle of a serving area with shelves and storage facilities: sometimes called a wagon.

Teetotal: refusing all drinks containing alcohol. The teetotal movement grew rapidly in the second quarter of the 19th century and faded rapidly after the First World War.

Temperance: advocating moderation in alcohol consumption and the avoidance of spirits. From the 1830's teetotalism gained ground.

Terracotta: very hard-wearing, unglazed pottery (Italian for baked earth).

Terrazzo: small pieces of marble set in concrete, rubbed down and polished. Usually used for flooring.

Index

Acknowledgements

The authors wish to acknowledge the following pub hunters (in alphabetical order) without whom we would have omitted some of the best pub interiors in this book:

John Adams, pub hunter extraordinaire
Hugh Armstrong
Mark Bravery
The late Andrew Clifton
John Crowhurst
John Cryne
Paul Dabrowski
Mark Hoile

Andy Hutton
Eric Martin
Daniel Meers
Steve Peck
Neil Pettigrew
Robert Preston
Kim Rennie
Gordon Scarfe
Roger Sedgley
Richard Seedhouse
Mick Slaughter
Bob Steel